the**GOD**lab

8 spiritual experiments you can try at home

Roger Bretherton

RIVER

River Publishing & Media Ltd
Barham Court
Teston
Maidstone
Kent ME18 5BZ

www.river-publishing.net

ISBN 978-1-908393-38-8

Typeset by Richard Weaver
Cover concept design by www.theres-a-thought.com
Author photograph by www.philhearingphotography.com
Printed and bound in the UK by CPI Anthony Rowe, Chippenham and Eastbourne

contents

dedication

To Gill

You remember that time on your eleventh birthday
When I accidentally threw your Frisbee into the sea?

(Sorry about that)

And then waded fully-clothed
Through the waves to rescue it?

Here's another attempt to rescue something
That matters to you.

I think this is the book you asked for.

I hope you like it.

God

(if you are there)

meet us

show yourself

end the darkness

bring the light

About the author

Dr Roger Bretherton is a Clinical Psychologist with special interest in psychotherapy. He is Senior Lecturer in Psychology at the University of Lincoln, and a popular speaker and workshop leader. He sits on the leadership of Elevate, the young adult expression of New Life Lincoln, is a venue and seminar leader at Grapevine International Celebration, and has recently joined the board of the national student network, Fusion. He is married to Marie-Claire, and they have two sons, Leo and Tom.

enter

begin

The God lab

I'd like to invite you to join me in the God Lab. It may be a familiar place to you. Most of us, at some point in our lives, find ourselves there – somewhere between believing and disbelieving. It's the waiting room where we often end up, neither sure of God's existence nor of his absence.

The God Lab is the place where we scan the heavens and launch probes into the ether in the hope of detecting a divine communication we can recognise. It's the place where hesitant and furtive prayers are uttered. It's the place where fragments of God's image are arranged and rearranged in an attempt to arrive at some collage that looks vaguely human. It's the place where rumours of angels are reported and friends share pet theories of life's meaning over coffee. The God Lab is anywhere when, against our better judgement, we find ourselves trying to strike a deal with heaven. It's not heaven and it's not really hell; it's more like purgatory. But we're all in it together – and it's fun.

The God Lab is not the sole preserve of the religious, nor does it exclude agnostics or sceptics – most of us seem to be there. Whether we say we believe or not, we cluster in factions around the work benches. It's not a place concerned with argument, but with experimentation. What's at stake in The God Lab is not the philosophical premise of God's existence, but whether he can be contacted, whether anyone can get hold of him.

I'm no expert in the God Lab. I'm working with the same battered apparatus as everyone else, messing about with some friends in a corner. But every now and then I get a result that seems pretty good to me – the spiritual equivalent of an exploding mushroom of gas, or a change in the colour of a flame, or a satisfying pop from the mouth of a test tube. And it makes me curious. I begin to wonder whether other people doing the same things get the same results. And that's where my invitation to the God Lab originates. I have a series of experiments you may like to try.

Knowing God is not a desk job

An experiment is, of course, a form of exploration. Instead of arguing endlessly about the way things are, we simply go and find out for ourselves. If we want to demonstrate decisively that the world is not flat, we set sail and hope there's no edge to fall off. Not everything can be learned in a stuffy lab. Some experiments require field work. Getting to know God is not a desk job.

This book is therefore a piece of practical spirituality – experimental discipleship, if you wish. It's about getting together with God. About finding our way home. About repairing a broken relationship, and perhaps healing our fragmentation.

It's a set of instructions rather than a work of theology or philosophy. It offers the kind of advice you'd be likely to get if you approached someone in the street and asked the way to the post office. Not a finely honed literary feast by any means, but a sharp and pointed set of directions.

When people ask me for directions in the street, I think hard. I point and wave my arms. I don't give every detail of the journey, I just mention the prominent landmarks along the way. Too much detail would confuse them; too little clarity would get them lost. And, by the time I've finished, I hope they know just enough to get there.

When it comes to finding our way to God, there's nothing quite like the direct approach. Rather than offering a set of beliefs to swallow or maxims to meditate, I'd rather just offer a series of instructions. You can decide whether to follow them or not. If you'd approached me in the street and asked the way to God, this is what I'd say.

In God's town we're all tourists

There are differences though, between directions in the street and directions in the spirit.

When I direct you to the post office, I'm usually not going there myself. You need to get there and I don't. I tell you and you walk away.

Giving directions to God, however, is more like realising we're both attempting to get to the same place and joining each other in the journey. I may start off trying to tell you how to find God in everyday life, but as I do, I get wrapped up in the search for God myself. I can't help it. Just talking about it reminds me how much I long for God. You've asked for directions to my friend's house and, in the middle of explaining where he lives, I recollect my fondness for him and that I haven't seen him for ages. So, with a degree of embarrassment, I not only direct you, but wonder if you'd mind if I came along too.

Being partial to God myself leaves me incapable of pointing you towards spiritual treasure without being ignited by the excitement of it myself. I'm too taken with the scenery of

God's country to be anything like a disinterested tour guide. In God's town, we're all tourists.

At home, when I tell you where the post office is, I know everything I need to know, you know nothing. I know where I am, you're the lost one. Directing people in the street could therefore leave me susceptible to a kind of patronising pride, whereby I take great pleasure in knowing where things are and imparting this knowledge to a poor lost stranger.

When giving directions to God, there's not much room for that kind of pride. It's true, I know a few things. I've pursued God for nearly two decades. I've had brushes with heaven and wrestlings with the divine. I know enough to point us in the right direction. But what I don't know far outweighs what I've been able to grasp so far. I know enough to have hope in the journey. I know that chasing God is worth it. I know it's rewarding. But I still have too much to learn to tower over you as an expert in the things of God. There's still a lot for us to explore together.

It could be that you're asking directions to God for the first time. It could be that you knew him once and now want to find your way back to something you're missing. Either way, if you feel lost and estranged from God, you're in good company. At times, I feel lost too. I've known the warm hearth of God's hospitality, but if I'm truly honest, it's a while since I've been willing to curl up in an armchair opposite him.

I don't feel abandoned as such, just distant. I still sense his presence at times, in my office and at home. I still experience a deep and gracious purpose unfolding in my otherwise average everyday life. But sometimes the snags and barbs of my personality obscure my vision of his goodness; the jagged edges of my character leave me disinclined to meet him face to face.

So I write not just with the aim of directing you, but in the hope that in doing so I might also trim back the hedge I've cultivated between myself and the God who loves me. I write just as much for myself as for anyone else. But I write in the hope that we both might share a beautiful journey into God.

Where is God?

In looking for God, Jesus can help us a great deal. In seeking spiritual direction, it can help to meet a consciousness greater than our own. We need to be stretched beyond what we currently know. Sometimes we need to stand on the shoulders of a spiritual giant and check out the view. We need someone to give us a leg up so we can peer over the garden wall of our present experience. Sometimes we need to learn at the feet of a religious genius. And Jesus, among other things, is definitely that.

Whenever I reflect on the historical period in which Jesus lived, I can't help being struck by the similarities between his time and ours.

We fail to understand Jesus of Nazareth unless we keep in mind that he was Jewish. Not only was *he* Jewish, but his mother was Jewish, his disciples were Jewish, and the vast majority of people he interacted with during his lifetime were Jewish. He belonged to the Jewish nation, Israel. This is important because when Jesus was around, in the first century AD, Israel was under Roman occupation and, generally speaking, they were pretty bemused about what God was up to. They believed themselves to be the chosen people of God and yet they were suffering under the heel of what they considered to be a godless empire. It was an intolerable contradiction.

Various factions at the time tried to explain the situation. Some believed that political cooperation with Rome was the best way of working things out. Some thought that nothing less than a revolutionary uprising would break the oppression. Still others sought deliverance in ethical and religious purity and awaited a supernatural rescuing direct from God. Others thought that this rescue had already happened secretly and retreated into the desert to live out a renewed nation in exile.

The average resident of first century Palestine could be forgiven for being confused. With so many voices clamouring to speak for God, it must have been difficult to know who to believe. It wasn't so much that God was absent, it was just hard to work out exactly what he was up to.

The Jewish theologian, Martin Buber, suggested that Western society is currently living through a similar eclipse of God. He hasn't gone missing, it's just that we've lost our capacity to perceive him. He hasn't hidden his face from us, we've lost our ability to recognise him.

And this eclipse seems to be culture-wide, with people in church on Sunday often struggling to perceive God just as much as those who spend Sundays at the golf course or the mall. The eclipse of God, to some extent, affects us all.

Of course, there are still some people in our culture of great spiritual experience and acumen. But, generally speaking, most of us feel pretty incompetent and clueless when groping our way through the spiritual undergrowth. We're not quite sure where to begin or whether we can trust ourselves to know that what we encounter is in any way real. Even if God is available to us, we don't know how to let him in.

The same question that echoed through Jesus' era, echoes through ours. Where is God?

Ask quietly

If we are asking that question though, we're often quite nervous about asking it too loudly. It puts us in a vulnerable position to publicly quest after God. Perhaps because there are so many people ready to give us *their* answer to it.

Some people would have us feel stupid for asking the question in the first place. If there is no God, then to persist in asking a meaningless question like this is just naivety. We're hankering after a childish illusion if we keep asking God for his whereabouts. We can therefore feel a bit foolish asking after God and may wish to conceal the fact that we're asking at all. But calling a question "stupid" doesn't make it go away, we just learn to keep it to ourselves.

Sometimes, attached to the fear of the question being stupid is a more profound fear: the fear of being disappointed by the answer.

At times the question, "Where is God?" is asked with a tinge of desperation. We want there to be a God. And for God to care. And for God to be knowable in some way. Behind the question of God's whereabouts can lie a painful yearning to find him and to be recognised by him. A yearning so painful, in fact, that we may not even dare admit it to ourselves, because the idea of there being no God – or worse still, a God who despises us – pours cold water on our deepest longings. Sometimes our fear of disappointment makes the search unbearable. But if God is there and we can know him, we have no choice but to bear the pain of calling for him.

We may also be reluctant to ask after God for fear of being duped. Just as in Jesus' day, there are numerous voices in ours ready to speak with absolute certainty on behalf of God. And if we are vulnerable enough to be searching openly for him, it's all too easy to be taken in by the first seemingly credible answer. To ask after God without reservation leaves us vulnerable to spiritual predators: cult leaders or money-minded empire builders. If we're not careful we can find ourselves jumping through religious hoops to get to God. And before we know it we're a long way from where we started, having adopted all kinds of foreign attitudes and behaviours, but having lost sight of our original simple passion to know God. We may fear to transparently search for God, in case we inadvertently swallow a lie in our hunger for the truth.

When the people of Jesus' day asked, "Where is God?" they were asking in a different way than we are today. They thought he existed, but didn't know what he was up to. We, on the other hand, are not even sure there is a God to be asked. The question isn't just an intellectual inquiry into his existence, but a call for him to make himself known in human experience. And, like them, we don't know which voices to listen to. We don't know where to turn for the answer, and this makes us nervous even to ask the question.

I make no threats

Jesus was one among many voices claiming to speak for God in his day. This is a helpful thought, because it allows us to rule out certain assumptions that can linger in the air when we consider Jesus.

One of those assumptions is that everything Jesus says is authoritative. In other words, all his words, as recorded by his biographers in the gospels, are absolute truth. They can't be quibbled with. They can't be debated. They can't be kicked about, thrown over, brought back, spun around, or hammered out. Unless, of course, all this spiritual wrestling is just a mock battle with a foregone conclusion, an elaborate courting ritual leading to our submission. We are told, before we even meet him, that Jesus is right and therefore we can only either swallow him whole or reject him utterly. This is an assumption I'd like us to suspend.

What would it be like if we'd never heard of Jesus? Never encountered Christians or church people? Never been told that he was divine or that we *had* to believe in him? Never been put under overt or implicit pressure to believe? What if you and I had lived as Jews in the northern part of first century Palestine and heard rumour of a travelling Rabbi called (like many other people we knew), Jesus?

Perhaps we would have been drawn to hear him speak by the gossip that reached our ears. The stories perhaps were intriguing, contradictory and exaggerated. He was a teacher, a healer, a storyteller, a psychic, an enigma. He had wisdom, he was funny, he was angry, he was mad. It would have been curiosity rather than obligation that compelled us to go and see this phenomenon for ourselves.

And when we (two faces in a crowd of thousands) heard him speak, we no doubt wondered what it all meant. Travelling home, and late into the night, we perhaps talked and debated what we made of him. Perhaps we wanted more and became his followers. Perhaps we decided it wasn't for us and returned to the daily grind with little thought for the horizon we once glimpsed. The point is that if we did come to the conclusion that Jesus was an authentic spokesperson for God, it would have been because we recognised it in him for ourselves, not because that opinion had been imposed on us beforehand.

Jesus was shockingly permissive in allowing people to make up their own minds about who he was. And the opinions differed: some loved him, some hated him, many were indifferent. Perhaps we could take the same permission – to make of Jesus and his role in our lives whatever we like, to form our opinions however we see fit, to position ourselves with regard to him in whatever way seems most authentic to us.

Without the freedom to reject something, we can never fully and wholeheartedly accept it. It's impossible to apprehend any truth with integrity when our agreement has been coerced.

Sometimes we take on opinions because they are fashionable or we fear the consequences of questioning the authorities who proffer them. Similarly with Jesus, there is very often an implicit threat in the invitation to believe in him – a threat that if we don't believe, there will be dire consequences.

I make no threats. If what I have to say about Jesus and his importance to your life makes no sense to you, I'm not going to scare you with stories of eternal damnation. If I fail to convince you that Jesus is worth knowing, I won't paint lurid pictures of hellfire hovering above your deathbed. My message is not so much "Love Jesus or else", but more like, "Meet Jesus and make up your own mind."

Attitudes we are to be

There are so many things to learn from Jesus that it's difficult to know where to start. Even if we want to check him out, we're often not quite sure how to do so. It therefore seems reasonable to start where he started.

His first public training programme was delivered over several days on a mountainside and is therefore nicknamed the Sermon on the Mount. In Matthew's gospel it takes up three chapters. It can be read in twenty minutes, but its scope is immense. It profiles the way of life that brings us into contact with God. It tells us how to be exuberant, how to relate to people, how to meet God in secret, how to approach our finances and decide the course of our lives. It's a training manual, but it's also an invitation – an invitation from Jesus to live the kind of life he lived. It's the distilled essence of what made him tick, delivered in the belief that it can make us tick too. He takes what he has and gives it to us freely.

The propositions that form the basis of our experiments are sketched out poetically in eight statements at the beginning of The Sermon. Like a piece of street poetry, they call us to order and grab our attention. They present us with a suck-it-and-see style of Christianity. They goad us to take the God stuff for a test drive. If read slowly and thoughtfully they become an invitation to explore, to taste and see.

Over the generations they've become known as the beautiful attitudes, or more simply, the beatitudes *(pronounced: BE-attitudes)* – the attitudes we are to *be*. Originally spoken in Aramaic, they can be translated into English as follows:

> Blessed are the poor in spirit, for theirs is the kingdom of heaven.
>
> Blessed are those who mourn, for they shall be comforted.
>
> Blessed are the gentle, for they shall inherit the earth.
>
> Blessed are those who hunger and thirst for righteousness, for they will be satisfied.
>
> Blessed are the merciful, for they will receive mercy.
>
> Blessed are the pure in heart, for they will see God.
>
> Blessed are the peacemakers, for they shall be called sons of God.
>
> Blessed are those who are persecuted for the sake of righteousness, for theirs is the kingdom of heaven.

They may not look like much, but the beatitudes are guiding lights for us. They have an ancient history. They've been pondered and pored over by saints, scholars and seekers for millennia. Anyone with serious business in the God Lab could do worse than to reckon with them. In them we can discover an acceptance from God and a way of knowing him that understands where we're coming from, that allows us to grow without expecting us to know it all from the start. Through the beatitudes, as we will see, Jesus invites us to meet God in real life.

Milestones of the spirit

These eight assertions are therefore experiments we can carry out in the God Lab. We'll look at them in detail in the chapters to come. But they're not disconnected quips. They form a sort of journey, a chain of coordinates to follow in exploring new territory. They mark out a pathway that many socks and sandals have trodden before us. They allow us to venture into God.

When I first started experimenting with the beatitudes in this way I found that these characteristics seemed to follow after one another. As I took on spiritual poverty, I found myself mourning over the pain in the world. As I took on compassion for the world around me, I found a groundedness, a centered-ness, overtook me, that I could only describe as humility. As my feet became more firmly planted on the ground, I found myself wanting to relate better to the world, to sort myself out, and more closely approximate the state that Jesus calls "righteousness". It was almost as if Jesus, speaking on a hillside two thousand years ago, had anticipated the milestones of my own spiritual growth. I was shaking hands with him across the ages and finding him in the here-and-now.

It seems to me that the beatitudes are milestones in the development of the spirit, just as sitting, crawling and walking are milestones in the development of the child. Each attitude is the fertile soil in which the next can take root. Like the ripples of a pebble in still water, each expanding circle makes room for the next.

Initially, I was nervous about talking openly about what I'd discovered. It seemed implausible to think that my own pilgrim-age had been marked out in the teaching of a previous era. It excited me, but I didn't want to tell anybody in case it sounded mad or just wrong. Later, I was reassured to discover that even great thinkers of the past, like Martin Luther and St Augustine, had discerned a similar pattern in the words of Jesus.

It could be that as you play with them you too discover a pathway that passes from one beautiful attitude to the next. Or maybe you don't. It doesn't really matter, it's only an experiment. You're free to approach your time in the God Lab with as much humour and curiosity as you care to muster. You can give it a shot and after that, whatever happens, happens.

Cairns on the mountainside

When I reflect on what the beatitudes can become for us, I get an image of rock piles or cairns on a mountain ridge.

I've often walked mountains in low cloud. Sometimes when the mist descends, I can barely see further than my next step. At others I can just make out the dark shape of the nearest landmark emerging from the gloom.

There is a tradition in the mountains of placing cairns along trails where walkers might lose their way. Each one starts as a small pile of stones, added to, year on year, by those who pass by, until they become landmarks in themselves. Some stones are placed out of whim, others out of gratitude, and still others for posterity or in memoriam. But as the cairns rise, they become the watchers, the guardians of the mountain, the custodians of unmarked paths. When the mist rolls through, or the snow falls, they stand as beacons on our way. They tell us we are not lost, nor are we alone, and many others have passed this way.

The attitudes Jesus endorses are like cairns – ancient markers or standing stones. They don't give us the whole picture as a map would, they just let us know where to go next. They don't require us to be virtuoso mountaineers, just wayfarers, adding more rocks to the pile. They allow us to be explorers, experimenters, nervous adventurers in the things of God. They invite us to extend ourselves and try a few new things in the God Lab.

bless

The cosmic emancipation project

Jesus chose to kick off one of his first public sermons with eight blessings. Over time they've come to be known as the *beatitudes* and, when looked at in depth, there seems to be some sort of progression to them. Once we set our minds to living out one of them we find the others quietly growing in us.

The beatitudes start at a comfortable pace. Jesus begins by blessing stuff I'm familiar with. He blesses spiritual incompetence. He blesses mourning and meekness. These are all attitudes I know. I recognise them. I can do them. But the incline gets steeper. By the end of the piece he's endorsing stuff like purity, peacemaking and endurance – the kind of attitudes that cause trouble; the sort of attitudes I rarely dare to adopt. At the start of the beatitudes following Jesus seemed easy, but by the end it looks impossible.

It makes me suspect that there's a secret hidden somewhere in these eight bite-sized blessings. Somewhere between the beginning and the end lies some magic. Whatever the secret is, it takes the weak-willed and fashions them into revolutionaries.

It mutates bewildered adherents into determined disciples. Somewhere on the journey, a transformation takes place. That's why I'm so taken with them. They offer me some hope that I can be different, that even a layabout like me can join the journey from sinner to sainthood. Even I can enlist in the procession from puerility to purity.

Not to put it mildly, I want God to break in and bring refreshment to my life. I want him to offer a way out of spiritual stagnation. Facing Jesus, I feel again the need to be saved; the need for an active God to pluck me out of my apathy; the need for a power greater than my own ambition to free me from the lethargy that contaminates almost everyone born into a culture that deifies comfort. I need saving from the triviality of my own concerns. I want to be liberated into a life of expansion and love.

If the beatitudes are some kind of spiritual growth plan, then this is the kind of human liberation project God has in mind. But how are we supposed to join the programme? If God loves us and has staged a rescue mission to free us, how can we cooperate with him in it? How do we enrol in the cosmic emancipation project?

More than just a courtesy call

Maybe I'm asking for too much, but I get the feeling that previous generations responded much more immediately to God than we do today. For them, relating to God came intuitively in a way that easily mystifies us.

The speed of modern life confronts us with such an avalanche of distraction that even the most profound spiritual revelations dissipate quickly. Too many things stimulate our desires and demand our money. A glimpse of God easily becomes just one more moment of exhilaration among others

– an exciting event that disappears without a trace. Communion with heaven can look like just another option during commercial breaks. We struggle to respond to God because we're response-weary, fed up of responding to emotive appeals.

Even the beatitudes could easily suffer the same fate and become yet another advertising slogan for brand-Jesus – their poetry and beauty holding our attention for a moment, but not long enough to make any real difference to us. Even if we believe them, or would like to believe them, we still don't always know what a sensible response would look like. We hear them and nod our heads, but our lives aren't changed. We can read them, but we often don't know what to do with them.

That's why I'd like to reformulate them as a set of experiments. I want to restate them in terms that make them somehow *do-able*.

If we want to access their power to shift the foundations of our existence and change the structure of our lives, we'll need to give them more than just a courtesy call. The eight spiritual experiments we're about to perform are a modest attempt to take the beatitudes seriously and get curious about what happens when we do.

Our work in the God Lab is therefore based on these eight verses which, when taken in the right way, claim to draw us into an experience of God. But how do we use eight ancient phrases as a basis for an experiential encounter with God in the here-and-now? If, through the words of Jesus, God is somehow extending his hand to us, how do we go about grasping it?

The secret oxygen

Looking at the beatitudes again, you'll undoubtedly notice a familiar pattern. Each one has a common structure.

> Blessed are the poor in spirit, for theirs is the kingdom of heaven.

Blessed are those who mourn, for they shall be comforted.

Blessed are the gentle, for they shall inherit the earth.

Blessed are those who hunger and thirst for righteousness, for they will be satisfied.

Blessed are the merciful, for they will receive mercy.

Blessed are the pure in heart, for they will see God.

Blessed are the peacemakers, for they shall be called sons of God.

Blessed are those who are persecuted for the sake of righteousness, for theirs is the kingdom of heaven.

First of all, each of them is a blessing.

When Jesus blessed the crowd he stood in a long tradition of powerful blessings. Many of the blessings in the history of the Jewish people had been recorded and still resonated in the identity of the nation. One of the them was the blessing spoken by their wisest ruler, King Solomon, at the opening of their first temple a thousand years earlier:

May the Lord bless you and keep you,

And make his face to shine upon you,

And be gracious to you,

And give you peace.

To be blessed, from this point of view, is to have God's attention and to live in the gleaming rays of his delight. It means freedom. It means living our lives under a graciousness that allows us to be, rather than constraining us into a tight mould we could never fit without injury.

Being blessed means the arrival of peace and rest in lives that are over-concerned, hectic and harrowing. It means God's voice, rather than damning and haranguing, addresses us with familiarity and fondness. It means that he cares for us, not as a means to an end, but as a unique treasure in our own right. The everyday blessings we hear are a shadow of the great blessing that surrounds us and underpins us, the secret oxygen of God's care and affection that is ours to breathe.

The heartbeat of God

But, for Jesus and the people he spoke to, blessing was even more than that. Blessing had what we would now consider legal ramifications. It wasn't just well-wishing, it had teeth.

Inheritance was passed from one generation to another by "blessing". Legal contracts or covenants expressed their terms and conditions through a series of blessings or curses that depended on the agreement being kept. Indeed the covenant, the legally binding contract, that Israel had signed up to with God, concluded with blessings for keeping the pact and curses for breaking it. In legal terms, to be blessed was to be permitted, or even entitled, to expect certain things – an inheritance or a relationship with God.

The crowd Jesus addressed must have had numerous concerns and interests. Some would have been sceptical, some curious, some miserable, others listless or doubtful. But when Jesus blesses them, he gives them permission to be as they are.

The same words are spoken to us too. He entitles us to be as we are. He dispels the painful self-consciousness that cramps our style. He waves away the resentment and discomfort that can make us squirm at the prospect of meeting God. He invites us into a bottomless and intelligent acceptance.

This may come as a surprise to us, because we might think that if God has anything to say, it's more likely to be criticism than blessing, judgement rather than acceptance. You may perhaps think that God is more interested in pointing out your flaws than commending your potential. But Jesus knows differently. Sitting on a hill, addressing anyone who's vaguely interested, his first words are, "You are blessed."

This is the essential background to all our experiments in the God Lab: God already accepts us as we are, even if we don't know it yet. The acceptance of God tells us that he's interested in us for what we bring. We each possess a wonderful uniqueness that he enjoys and wishes to be in relationship with. He knows us and accepts us. This is what experimenting in the God Lab is all about: coming to know God's acceptance in our own experience.

Blessing, therefore, hangs over all eight beatitudes like a glittering cloud waiting to be called down by a receptive attitude. Blessing is the roof that sits over them under which we can make ourselves at home. It's the ground beneath all eight verses where we can stand securely. Blessing underpins every step of our spiritual adventure with Jesus, allowing us to be confident and intrepid in scouting out God's country.

All the beatitudes are blessings. Each is a gesture of divine goodwill, a thumbs up from the Almighty, a reassuring nod from heaven. Blessing is their overarching, undergirding, all-encompassing atmosphere. Jesus rhythmically taps out the heart-beat of God towards us: BLESSED, BLESSED, BLESSED ...

God's enthusiastic "yes" to us is the beginning and end of everything Jesus represents.

I'm glad *you're* here

Blessing is good, but it can be vague. A divine blessing could be used as a way of covering over the details of our lives – the equivalent of being on a distant relative's Christmas card list. We suspect he likes us, but as he never sees us, we don't know what *exactly* he likes about us. We fear he may not like us if he *knew* us.

It's only as I examine the content of the beatitudes that I realise Jesus really is blessing *me*. In fact, the more I reflect on them, the more I imagine that he was reading the hearts of the people stood in front of him. Could it be that he caught the eye of a passionate, but bewildered young man and blessed his emptiness? Did he spot a widow surrounded by her children and bless her grieving? Did he catch sight of a weary farm hand and bless his connection to the earth? As Jesus spoke these statements, he looked into the eyes of the people before him and said, "I'm glad *you're* here." They were general invitations for everyone, but they confront each of us with the notion that we have a place in God's affections.

And the characteristics Jesus blesses aren't harsh demands to make ourselves more acceptable by becoming something foreign to what we are. If they're demands at all, they only demand that we become more fully ourselves. If there is a transformation to be had, it's a return to an earlier innocence we once abandoned. Jesus' blessings identify us and tell us that God is with us in our uniqueness. Through his words, God strides like King Arthur to every willing soul, naming us, knighting us and calling us to arise.

Each blessing comes attached to a particular attitude. Jesus seems to be saying that attitudes like gentleness, purity or mercy can open us up to the goodness God wishes to pour into our lives. They act as skylights on heaven through which sunshine can stream. They aren't conditions of God's love, but windows to experiencing it.

Play with other ways of seeing

An attitude is a state of the entire person. It's the position we choose to adopt towards our situation. Changing our attitude changes our way of being in the world. When we alter our attitude we redecorate our mind; it gives us a different take on the same circumstances. Different attitudes allow us access to different realities.

If we step out of the front door wearing an attitude of acceptance, the world occurs to us very differently than if we venture out with a scathing disposition. Our attitude determines what we notice, or fail to notice, and what we make of what we see.

An open attitude allows us to see an apology as an attempt to repair a relationship. A closed attitude inclines us to view it as a selfish attempt to avoid awkwardness. A critical attitude isn't satisfied by anything but the most degrading of apologies. A cautious attitude waits before drawing any conclusion at all. Our attitude at any given moment is the psychological atmosphere we breathe. It's the way we hold ourselves, the lens through which we view and create reality.

Most of us live with a fairly limited and familiar set of attitudes. We have a few firm favourites that have probably worked for us in the past and we stick with them. Occasionally we may experiment with other ways of being, but generally speaking, the world we see through our limited repertoire of attitudes is what we call reality. What we see isn't wrong, it just isn't everything. There's more to see. And seeing more requires us to play with new ways of seeing.

Yet changing our attitude isn't always easy – particularly the attitudes that protect us. Attitudes based on fear of being taken for a ride, or misled, or betrayed, or hurt, have often served us so well that it seems insane to consider exchanging them for what appears to be a dangerous naïveté.

Our caution-based attitudes do protect us, but they can also isolate us. Our fear of being taken in by a scam sometimes excludes us from being taken in out of the rain. It not only prevents people getting to us, but prevents us from getting to people. This isn't to advocate we lower all our defences, but rather that we consider at least the prospect of allowing some openness to new things. Even when the siege is on, we may still allow ourselves the space to ponder the words of a messenger from enemy lines.

The range of attitudes we're prepared to experiment with is often determined by our understanding of what life is about and the part we play in it. If the world is a competitive jungle in which only the fittest and fastest survive, then those who wish to distinguish themselves can hardly fail to adopt attitudes consistent with the pitiless battle for survival. And anyone who suggests otherwise is rightly accused of not living in the "real world". We arrive at, and stick with, our attitudes based on what we're trying to achieve in life. Our agenda determines our attitudes.

There could be more

To suggest therefore that we should experiment with attitudes not normally familiar to us, is to suggest experimenting with an alternative lifestyle. Road testing different attitudes is like sampling different meanings of life. The next few chapters invite you to do exactly this. To look at the eight attitudes Jesus blesses; to get a "feel" for them – a sense of what it would be like to live in the atmosphere described.

But there could be more. Each beatitude is a promise: if you take this way of viewing life, you'll make space for something good to come your way. They leave us open and receptive. And when we take them on, we offer God a hospitable atmosphere in which to make himself at home. They free our hands so we can catch the gifts he's poised to throw at us.

Your sense of these attitudes could become a way of stumbling into a God who loves you. The question to be tested in the God Lab is whether taking the attitudes commended by Jesus, brings us into this knowledge of God's blessing. Do these attitudes allow us to perceive a reality that was previously invisible to us?

What to look out for

Each beatitude therefore contains a blessing and an attitude. Each one also ends with a consequence.

A consequence isn't a reward. It's not a pat on the head or a trinket for doing as we're told. It's the predictable outcome of living a particular way. In the beatitudes, it's what happens when we adopt an attitude with the intention of meeting with God. If I cross the room to open a window, fresh air flows in. The fresh air isn't a reward for "window-openers" such as myself, it's just what happens when I open a window.

Each of the attitudes that Jesus names is an open window through which the fresh air of blessing can blow into our lives. But they also give us a clue as to what we might expect from God if we incline ourselves towards him in a certain way. They say, for example that mourners will be comforted, peacemakers recognised and the merciful shown mercy. This is a reality we may have previously missed. Jesus tells us what to look out for if we carry ourselves with a certain bearing towards God. He tantalises us with a multi-coloured realm of blessing waiting to be explored.

The sky comes all the way to the ground

One of these outcomes is repeated in the beatitudes. It's promised to us twice, at the beginning and the end, in the first statement and the last. In the first beatitude, Jesus says the kingdom of heaven belongs to the spiritually poor. In the last, he says it belongs to those who are persecuted. It leaves us wondering what exactly the kingdom of heaven is and why it's offered to us, not once, but twice in the beatitudes.

Given the political history of Western Christianity, it's almost impossible to hear a phrase like "kingdom of heaven" without calling to mind crusaders and empire builders. The kingdom of heaven with its imperialistic connotations is hardly a welcome concept to most people. It's been used to justify bloodshed. Entire armies have marched to war claiming to defend its interests. When Jesus offered it to the poor and the persecuted, this can hardly have been what he had in mind.

The kingdom of heaven is *the* signature theme of everything Jesus did. When he toured the towns and villages of first century Palestine, his fundamental message was laugh-out-loud simple: change your mind and accept that the kingdom of heaven, the God-stuff, is here-and-now. He wasn't some dreary, placard-wearing (repent for the end is nigh) bore. He was saying that the things of God are ready for us, now.

Very simply put, the kingdom of heaven is all the stuff of God.

Or to put it another way, I watched my son Leo drawing a picture with pencil crayons last week. He's four, so he's only just learned to draw. And having filled the paper with a balloon, a horse and the sun, he suddenly realised he'd missed out the sky. Picking up a blue crayon, he furiously scribbled a narrow band of blue at the top of the page. And it reminded me that I used to draw the sky like that: a thin blue line, separated from the ground, out of reach, high above the sun and everything else. Until one day an art teacher at school asked me to look out of the window and notice that the sky wasn't really a blue stripe above my head. If I looked closely I'd notice that the sky and the ground always meet at the horizon. "The sky," she said, "comes all the way down to the ground."

I mentioned earlier that, generally speaking, the Jewish people Jesus addressed didn't doubt the existence of God. They just wondered when he was finally going to show up and rescue them from military occupation. They wanted God to act definitively in real time and save the day. So, when Jesus announced the kingdom of heaven to his countrymen, he was telling them that the action of God they'd been waiting for had finally arrived. God would now act in the world. The hurricane of heaven had made landfall. The sky comes all the way to the ground.

Unfortunately, it didn't look much like the military campaign they'd been expecting and consequently, accepting the action of God in their lives involved a considerable rewriting of their expectations. There's a lesson for us here. Whenever we wish to apprehend God, we should be ready to be surprised by what we find. More often than not, God turns out to be better than we assumed him to be.

The catch-all phrase

The kingdom of heaven is a highly inclusive concept. It's not the church, it's anywhere and everywhere that God is active and up to something. It's in answers to prayer and friendships repaired. It's where justice and fairness win out and peace is restored. It includes healing of body and mind, and cleansing of the conscience. It includes wisdom and laughter in living.

The kingdom of heaven is the catch-all phrase for all the things that God is doing in the world. Any time you think you've had a brush with God, you've stumbled over a boundary into the kingdom of heaven. The better we know God, the easier it is to notice the hallmarks of his working. According to Jesus, however, if we want to catch more than a snapshot of the kingdom in passing, we'll need a change of lens – an alteration of mind.

That's what the beatitudes offer us.

They begin and end with the promise that the kingdom of heaven is ours. Like bookends on a shelf, these two promises hold together everything in between. If each beatitude is a milestone in a spiritual growth curve, then the first affords us a promissory glimpse of the things of God, and the last a permanent dwelling in awareness of the divine. If the first step allows us to see God, the last allows us to see nothing but God.

The beatitudes don't insist that we dive headfirst into the spiritual deep end. They slowly lower us into the waters of God-consciousness. Adopting each attitude draws us further into sharing God's passion for the world. We may begin concerned only for ourselves, but the pathway leads us beyond self-concern to engagement with the world, even to the point of suffering in order to care. The beatitudes therefore meet the litmus test of any genuine spiritual journey – not just whether it transforms us, but whether it allows us to be the change we want to see in the world.

Finding our place in the kingdom of heaven in the here-and-now is the big promise at the beginning of Jesus' first sermon. It's an invitation to participate in the godly magic that leaves nothing it touches unchanged. The kingdom of heaven therefore sums up what happens when we start to take the beatitudes to heart.

Skip to the end

We're therefore almost ready to turn the page and start work in the God Lab. But just before we do, one last thing.

Every year I supervise psychology students conducting research on members of the public. Quite a lot of this research seems to involve asking relative strangers to do things they ordinarily wouldn't do: look at strange photos, fill out personal questionnaires, follow dots on a computer screen, or wear metal apparatus on their heads. Psychology research is like that.

Thankfully, before our students are even allowed to breathe in the vicinity of a potential research participant, they're also required to complete an ethics form, just to make sure no one gets hurt. One of the most important sections in the form concerns consent. In other words, before people get involved, do they know what they're letting themselves in for and, if it turns out they don't like it, can they get out?

There's no real danger involved in the God Lab, but in the spirit of informed consent it might help you to know what's going to happen next. The eight chapters that follow take the beatitudes one by one. Each chapter contains a bit of explanation from me, followed by the experiment and some concluding remarks. You can read through the whole thing and decide whether you wish to try it out or not.

However, as I mentioned at the beginning of the chapter, the beatitudes themselves become more demanding as they go on. This is also true of the experiments. Just as the beatitudes increase in intensity, so too do the experiments. For this reason, the chapters can be read individually and you can opt out at any time.

The final section of the book is called "exit". So if at any point you decide you've had enough or that it's all getting a bit too intense, the fire escape is clearly marked. You're free to withdraw at any point – just skip to the end, I'll meet you there.

Chasing God's coattails

The great saints and mystics of the past took their relationship with God exceptionally seriously. They approached prayer and meditation with the same systematic attitude we'd apply to developing a new technology. They're the past-masters of the God Lab, painstakingly exposing themselves to the joys and traumas of chasing God's coattails. Knowing God isn't an exact science, but it is possible to apply ourselves to it methodically. That's what we're going to do now.

We therefore have a working hypothesis to test in the laboratory of our experience. We have eight of them in fact. Eight poetic assertions from Jesus. Each is a blessing. Each endorses an attitude. Each entails a promise. And each invites us to enter the God Lab with a simple question in mind: if we believe his words just enough to try them, do they work?

experiment

open

The chase was on

I first got serious about making contact with God when I was sixteen. At the time I had a part-time job working in a photocopy shop and spent every Saturday printing documents, sending faxes, fixing typewriters and selling stationery. It wasn't the best job in the world, but in the end it paid for my driving lessons, so it was worth it.

It also played an unusual role in my spiritual development. On top of everything else, the shop was a hub for a book recycling scheme. People would arrive with huge crates full of paperback books and heave them over the counter to my boss. He'd take them out to the stock cupboard in the back and sort them out. Some were binned, others were re-sold for local charities. But, while they passed through the shop, I was welcome to take anything interesting that caught my eye among the tattered volumes.

One of the books I took from those dusty boxes became the inspiration for much of my adventuring with God. It was called *The Pursuit of God* by A. W. Tozer. I now know that he was actually a fairly famous preacher and mystic in the early part of the 20th Century, but at the time I'd never heard of him. I just liked the sound of the book.

Reading it for me was like being set on fire. The prayers and exercises he outlined somehow carried me into an experience of God I'd previously not known. I now knew that God could be pursued. The chase was on.

Spiritual explorations in secret

Over the next few years I drew inspiration from reading the lives of saints and spiritual adventurers – people who made it their business to shake God by the lapels until he listened. They heard God's voice. They saw prayers answered. And they distilled what they'd learned into nuggets of spiritual wisdom – small experiments to try out in the laboratory of prayer.

These are the experiments I picked up on. My desire to meet God was so keen that I started trying them everywhere: in bed at night, on the train to town, in empty classrooms at school, out dancing with friends, anytime I was alone. No one knew what I was up to, not even my closest friends. And apart from the occasional comment that I was slightly more peaceful than normal, I doubt anyone guessed. The findings of these experiments were thrilling for me, but it seemed important to keep them to myself. They felt somehow forbidden, secret, intimate even. I knew I'd come to know God, but I didn't tell anyone.

Perhaps it's best to start our spiritual explorations in secret. If we want to meet with God, it's maybe better to keep mum. It'll help us avoid embarrassment if our spiritual enthusiasm turns out to be no more than a flash in the pan. It gives us time to ponder our experiences before explaining them to anyone else. It allows our spiritual muscles to strengthen before lifting any weight.

This is the paradox: opening ourselves to God often involves hiding ourselves away.

The first experiment in the God Lab is therefore an experiment in "openness", a lesson in spiritual availability. It's the first attitude Jesus commends to us in the beatitudes and (again) it reads like this:

> Blessed are the poor in spirit,
>> for theirs is the kingdom of heaven.

Unfortunately for us, the first beatitude is also the most incomprehensible. We don't really use phrases like "poor in spirit" or "kingdom of heaven" in everyday language, so it may not make much sense to us.

In the previous chapter I said a bit about the kingdom of heaven being the stuff of God. So we have some idea of what we're being promised. Jesus is inviting us to begin a living exploration of God. All very well. But what is poverty of spirit? And how can we turn it into an experiment worth trying?

It looks like I have some explaining to do.

What we're like

We rarely use words like "spirit" in everyday conversation. We may talk about *team spirit* or describe a good friend as a *generous spirit*. But when we do we're not talking about a *thing* called a spirit, attached to a team or a person. We usually just mean the general sense, the atmosphere that surrounds a winning team or a lively character. We therefore talk about spirit without being expressly religious or spiritual.

This way of talking about spirit is probably quite close to Jesus' intention in using the word. We may struggle to understand "poverty of spirit" as an everyday phenomenon, but when Jesus addressed his first century audience, they almost certainly knew what he was talking about. Some of his parables and sayings may have been confusing to them at times, but I don't think this was one of them.

What would be the point of blessing the crowd in terms they couldn't understand? Surely one of the rules of giving compliments is that we must at least understand what we are being complimented for. So too with blessing. When Jesus blessed the crowd for their poverty of spirit, they knew what he was getting at. He was speaking in plain language about things they could recognise in everyday life. They wouldn't have needed formal theological training to get it.

Unfortunately, we've inherited centuries of talk about spirits and souls as invisible appendages on our bodies. As a result, when we think of spirit, we imagine a ghostly aura that follows us wherever we go, or a bubble-like halo rising over our heads like a solar flare, or a will-o'-the-wisp, hidden in the heart waiting to depart with our final breath. These are fine poetic images and therefore contain some truth, but they mislead us if we want to detect spirit in everyday living. These images can be a bit spooky. They mislead us by making spirit something alien or magical – the kind of entity best depicted by a Hollywood special effect, rather than a normal and recognisable part of us, of any human being. These images leave us looking in the wrong place for our spirit, as if it's something external, a ghost that follows us around, rather than an everyday component of our existence.

We may not be able to say what spirit looks like, but we know what it's like to have one. Our spirit is our ability to move beyond ourselves; to step outside ourselves. It's what we might call the human capacity for self-transcendence. It allows us to reach into the past and understand civilisations that existed thousands of years ago, to imagine future possibilities, to soar all over the universe in our imagination.

Our ability to transcend ourselves allows us to imagine much more than we can see with our eyes. It lets us empathise with other people as we consider what it would be like to be them. It affords us creativity and initiative when we act to bring our dreams into reality. It allows us humour when finding subversive perspectives on the ironies of life. It lets us laugh at the faintly ridiculous deficit between who we are and who we'd like to be. As far as we can tell, this capacity for transcending the self, of all the species on the planet, is most highly developed in human beings. It's one of the features that makes us recognisably human and it's what we refer to when we talk about "spirit".

Defining spirit as our capacity to move beyond ourselves makes it no longer the sole preserve of religion or spirituality. The capacity for self-transcendence is demonstrated by everybody all the time. And if this is what we mean by "spirit", then every time we hear a joke, witness an argument, view a piece of art, write a love letter, take a moment to think, play a board game or listen to a friend, we encounter something spiritual. The moment we define spirit as "the ghost in the machine", it becomes foreign, uncanny, inhuman and unrecognisable. Once the ghost is exorcised, we see that everything is spiritual. The boundaries between the spiritual and the physical, the human and the divine, blur. Spirit is what connects the core of our being with everything else.

Our spirit is therefore in operation when we reflect on ourselves. It's the capacity to stand back and take a look at our lives. It's the way we know ourselves, direct our lives and draw conclusions about who we are. Spirit as the capacity to self-transcend is our relationship to ourselves. Not how we define ourselves in words, but how we relate to those definitions. Other people experience our spirit when they relate to us. It's how we come across, the vibe we give off, the atmosphere we inhabit. Our spirit sums us up. It's how we are. It's *what we're like.*

Willing to change our minds

It's therefore a surprise that Jesus blesses *poverty* of spirit. Surely *richness* of spirit is a more admirable trait? We look up to people who are full of self-confidence, who need nothing but their own permission to be who they are. Jesus is opposing this kind of self-possession only to the extent that it deceives us into thinking we can survive entirely alone. In its extreme form it cuts the cord of relationship between ourselves and the rest of the world. It makes us impregnable to love and is therefore incompatible with knowing God.

Richness of spirit, taken to its logical conclusion, is to be full of ourselves. To be certain, ruthless and unyielding. To be rich in spirit is to believe we have a lock on the truth and no longer need to consider other points of view – so entrenched in defending our position that we no longer tolerate questions or disagreement. We are rich in spirit whenever we feel full of our own ideas and ambitions to the exclusion of everything else. To be rich in spirit is to be closed, rigid and proud; to allow the warm waters of the spirit to freeze into an icy solid.

Of course, we all have areas of rigidity like this. We all have icebergs floating in our inner oceans: prejudices, assumptions, knee-jerk reactions. But, according to Jesus, God can't be found in rigid adherence to particular doctrines. Nor in the suspicion of slamming doors and turning locks. He unequivocally rejects a narrow individualism that despises the rest of the world while clinging to cast iron principles. In the first beatitude, Jesus fundamentally opposes fundamentalism.

Instead, he commends the virtue of openness as the gateway to knowing God. It's in an attitude of openness and hospitality that we can find him. Poverty of spirit isn't low self-esteem or lack of backbone, but a simple acknowledgement that we don't have it all nailed down and can therefore hear the needs and opinions of others. Poverty of spirit, among other things means being available to others and responsive to the world. A recognition that we're not totally self-sufficient.

When it comes to God, spiritual poverty is the willingness to hear his call; the willingness to recognise that we may be wrong about him; that many of our notions of God fall short of grasping what he's really like. Poverty of spirit is a willingness to accept our opinions and beliefs as provisional and potentially alterable. To be poor in spirit is to be willing to change our minds.

Stop and take stock

Changing our minds though doesn't just mean modifying our intellectual or political opinions. It's an inclination to re-examine the thoughts and intentions that govern our daily life. It refers to what we might call social cognition: our thoughts about the people and situations we negotiate each day. Poverty of spirit is a willingness to carry ourselves with responsiveness and flexibility in everyday living.

Perhaps you have a plan, a strong, driven sense of where you'd like to get to in life; an ambition that dictates what you're prepared to acknowledge, or ignore, in your propulsion towards success.

On the other hand, maybe you had a plan once, but now find yourself in a hiatus? The plan failed, the ambition faltered, the dream died, and now you're not quite as certain as you used to be, not quite sure who to blame or what to do next. Openness to God often comes easier to us when stuck in a moment like this than when we're driving ourselves relentlessly towards renown.

We may think we're pursuing an urgent, essential goal, and therefore can't tolerate even the slightest interruption in our meteoric rise. But the challenge of openness requires us to take time to stop, to think and reflect. It's easy to justify ignoring

God's voice. The voice of conscience that calls us back to ourselves is quickly drowned by the white noise of daily necessities. Poverty of spirit therefore implies a willingness not just to change our minds, but to turn and attend to the glimmers of illumination we may otherwise push past in our determination to get on.

This is why we need Jesus to bless us at the outset – to tell us we're accepted and okay; to let us know that God smiles knowingly at our attempts to make sense of it all. We need his blessing, because some of us fear to stop even for a moment. Our minds have been so filled since childhood with exhortations to hurry up, move along, and stop wasting time that it seems unforgivable to allow ourselves a moment of rest.

Some of us have kept going by telling ourselves that ultimate success and satisfaction lie just around the next corner. But each corner, once turned, unveils yet another corner. The myth that contentment is found just around the next bend begins to fade, as does our strength to continue. We need to be blessed because we need to know we can trust the instinct that tells us it's time to stop and take stock. We need to allow ourselves permission to do nothing at times, even if, to begin with, it feels wrong. We need to know that rest is commended to us by God, even if it feels wicked and awkward to us.

The ability to stop, reflect and change direction is implied by Jesus when he blesses poverty of spirit.

The possibility of faith

If openness involves pausing for thought, it therefore also requires us to let our guard down.

We often have a strong resistance not just to the idea of God, but to doing anything that looks like a move in the direction of relating to him. The world has come to believe that God is non-existent, or at least absent from life as we know it, and it therefore seems the height of stupidity to start praying to the void above our heads. Breaking the silence by speaking into empty space can make us feel absurd.

If there is no God we're right to feel silly when we pray. Instead, we should strengthen ourselves. We should harden ourselves against the deep sense of insignificance provoked by contemplating the vast empty spaces of the universe. Not only must we learn to live without God, but we have to give up wanting him to exist in the same way that children give up comfort blankets.

In a world without God, maturity means facing his non-existence, fortifying ourselves against an ambivalent universe and purging ourselves of any desire to turn back and seek again the childish comforts of a heavenly father. To be an adult is to no longer need God.

The problem is that sometimes we find ourselves wanting to pray. Perhaps a prayer of last resort promoted by tragedy, or a prayer of thanks for friendship, or beauty, or the birth of a child. Sometimes, when we're alone, we find ourselves just wanting to talk to God, but we're not really sure if anyone's listening, and perhaps feeling that our voices sound faintly ridiculous hanging in the air.

When the impulse to pray strikes us, it can occur as a temp-tation to be overcome. We tell ourselves that we're too old for that kind of thing; that it's weak to turn to God, when we can get on and solve most of our problems ourselves. In a godless universe, prayer is reserved for the weak and dependent, and the more we pride ourselves on self-sufficiency, the less likely we are to succumb to the temptation to pray.

We therefore find all kinds of resistance and criticism arising in us when we consider praying. Nothing could be simpler than speaking to God, but nothing is resisted so firmly because of its implications. We muzzle ourselves. The threshold from not-praying to praying is often locked and barred with a steel door.

This resistance may occur to us as an aversion – a simple unwillingness to cross the invisible line into prayer. Openness, I guess, ultimately involves being willing to cross the line. It means simply acknowledging, whether we care to admit it or not, that we still need God. Poverty of spirit is therefore not faith, but an openness to the possibility of faith.

Spiritual incompetence

Even if we do cross the line and cautiously offer a prayer or two, our problems don't end there. Sometimes when we pray to God alone, or visit church, we assume that he needs us to be more than we are – that he won't accept us unless we put on airs and graces; unless we morph ourselves into something other than what we know ourselves to be. We may prefer to avoid contact with God because he leaves no room for what really matters to us. He seems interested in our presence, but not in our personality. He knows the number of hairs on our head, but doesn't care what colour we dye them.

In the first beatitude, Jesus floats the possibility that God may have been misrepresented to us. Perhaps by the religious authority figures we've rubbed shoulders with. In blessing openness, he's inviting us to find out for ourselves whether God really is the way we've been told he is. To adopt an open-ness of spirit is to allow for the possibility that God may be different from the person we were threatened with in Sunday school. An open spirit doesn't require us to believe that there is a God like this, just to acknowledge that there may be.

Could it be that God isn't looking for people who can offer him a seamless performance? What if being able to perform perfectly for God is actually a form of spiritual closedness, an attempt to replace him rather than work with him? The more polished our religion becomes, it seems, the less space it leaves for God.

Religious self-righteousness is therefore the specific form of spiritual "wealth" that Jesus dismisses in this beatitude. The relief to be had with his blessing spiritual poverty is that most of us are already where he'd like us to be. It means that if we come to pray and don't know what to say, then we're right where we should be. We can say that we don't know what to say. We can begin by saying we don't know where to begin. We can know that God loves and respects the integrity of this kind of praying and delights to show himself to people who offer him anything resembling an open door. What looks to us like spiritual incompetence, God accepts as a gift: our willingness to take the risk of opening ourselves to him.

The first experiment, therefore, is about opening ourselves to God. It simply tests the hypothesis that an attitude of openness allows us to meet God. It's time to take a look at it.

The bare bones

This experiment is therefore similar to those I followed as a teenager. Since then it's become my habitual way of checking-in with God. It frequently offers me moments of deep spiritual connection that I return to time and again. It's especially helpful for getting into the right mindset for longer or more intense periods of prayer, and with practice can be done very quickly almost anywhere. Sometimes ten seconds is more than enough time to close my eyes and drop in on God.

These are the bare bones of the experiment.

Experiment I:

Find somewhere quiet, comfortable and without distractions for the first few times you try this. It can be done anywhere, but to begin with you may like to make some space to be alone.

Set yourself a time limit. Ten minutes is probably enough to begin with. Not so much time that you get bored or distracted. You can extend this time later if you'd like to. It's better to end wanting more than to go on too long. I know some people who can do this exercise for hours.

Sit in an armchair or kneel comfortably. You may wish to adopt an open posture, with palms upward as if to receive a gift, or allow a slight smile to form on your lips.

Close your eyes and enjoy a few moments of silence, taking some slow deep breaths.

When you feel ready and receptive, say the word "blessed" gently and decisively. You can speak it aloud or silently in your mind. Imagine Jesus on the hillside two thousand years ago, speaking this word over ordinary people. Remember that this is God's word to you, here and now. You are blessed.

Allow the word to resonate in the silence and then, after a short pause, speak it again gently but firmly. Don't rush. If you find yourself getting distracted, don't criticise yourself for it, just return to the word "blessed".

You may like to experiment with variations on the theme. You can speak the word "blessed" in different directions: to yourself, to God, to the world around you. It's a simple affirmation of what is.

Notice any images that form in your mind in response to the blessing. You may see a warm light like the sun beaming down on you, or experience physical sensations of warmth or tingling, laughter or tears. If so, don't hold on to these experiences too tightly. Continue with the word blessed and enjoy whatever pleasurable images or sensations occur.

If, at the end of your time, there are things you'd like to say or ask God, feel free to speak them out. Don't expect an answer, just leave them there for the time being.

Like any experiment, this exercise is not a one-stop-shop. You'll need to repeat it to get the best out of it.

Don't be surprised if your first few attempts are pretty unimpressive or even difficult. I've repeated it thousands of times, several times a day, and the results have been variable. Sometimes meditating on blessing is no more than five minutes in which I enjoy thinking nice thoughts. Sometimes it produces spontaneous mental images, prayers or decisions.

On rare occasions, I've sometimes found the experiment takes a strange and unexpected turn. The atmosphere of the room intensifies, my ears ring, my skin burns and electricity crackles through the air. Afterwards, people who don't know what I've been up to say my face shines. Or my office is filled with peace. Or my apartment has a benevolent presence.

I have my moments. Who knows what will happen if you try it.

Prepared to wait for God

In the first beatitude then, Jesus said that the kingdom of heaven belongs to the *poor in spirit*. The God-stuff belongs to anyone who's available to it. If we dare to seek relationship with God, we will find it. An attitude of openness offers fertile ground for the friendship to germinate.

When I was ten years old, a friend down my street was given a CB radio for Christmas. We were really excited. After school we'd rush to his house to listen to the traffic on his headset. Unfortunately, not much happened on the radio waves in our town, so we spent most of our time broadcasting into static, hoping someone would hear us. Every now and then, a distorted voice – usually some trucker on a nearby motorway – would crackle out of the white noise and greet us, only to disappear again into the silence. Those moments of contact entranced us and made the waiting worth it.

Living in openness to God is a bit like leaving our CB radios on, just in case. It's like leaving the landing light on for a loved one or the door ajar so good friends can pop in. Living in openness is being prepared to wait for God. As I said earlier, it's not faith, but it allows for the possibility of faith.

share

अध्याय

Liquid prayer

Many of my most intimate encounters with God have happened in grief. Like the time a close friend died of cancer in her twenties. Or when a client committed suicide. Or when an earthquake hit one of the poorest countries on the planet. Or when I lost the grandmother I hadn't visited for fifteen years. In all these tragic moments, I followed a primal impulse to hide away and invite God to join me in the pain. And in moments like these I came to understand why one great writer called tears *liquid prayer.*

There's an unavoidably tragic dimension to life and any spirituality worth its salt looks this dark side of life square in the face. It can't be finessed or avoided, it can only be acknowledged. And while some people seem to sneak smoothly through life without ever alerting the forces of mishap to their existence, most of us find that sooner or later tragedy straddles our path and demands its due.

Jesus wasn't ignorant of pain. His life was marred in many ways by the trials and sorrows of human existence, and his death was nothing if not torturous. The fact that he somehow brought a contagious exuberance to the task of living isn't to say that he discovered some mysterious way of floating above the undertow of human misery. He was a man of sorrows and well acquainted with grief, but he also danced and laughed and sang for all he was worth. Somehow he'd learned to tap deep inner wells of hope even in the teeth of despair. Somehow joy and trauma linked arms in the bittersweet life of Jesus of Nazareth.

So when, in the second beatitude, he says …

> Blessed are those who mourn,
> for they will be comforted.

… it wasn't a bland platitude issued from an ivory tower. It wasn't the musing of an armchair philosopher. It was a tried and tested promise from a man who knew pain and would know much more before his time was up.

Grief wears many guises

In the first beatitude Jesus blessed openness. He commended responsiveness. He revelled in our willingness to be affected by life rather than holding ourselves aloof from it. This kind of openness, he suggested, allows us to cooperate with what God is up to in the world. But once we take on this kind of openness we begin to realise that it comes at a price. To be open and aware of the world around us heightens our sense of the pain we encounter there. It inclines us to feel the pain of other people. In this way poverty of spirit evolves into mourning, for ourselves and for the world.

In the second beatitude, therefore, Jesus speaks into the apparently pointless suffering that you and I may see or live through, and lends it some dignity by blessing our attempts to come to terms with the pain. When tragedy strikes unpredictably, we may be at our wits end, at a loss for what to do or who to turn to. But Jesus tells us that in our moments of mourning, God has something for us.

Mourning is the way we respond to loss. Whenever we lose anything that really matters to us we grow sad and grieve. Not surprisingly then, most of us associate mourning with death – usually of someone close to us. We may have known them well or just admired them from a distance. It may have been a relative we struggled to relate to, or a dear friend who knew our deepest secrets. Whoever they were, mourning tells us that they mattered to us.

Grief therefore wears many guises, some of which strike us as strange and unexpected. It can be tinged with gratitude as we celebrate a life well lived, or laced with regret as we rehearse the words that went unsaid, or spiked with anger as we rue the unfinished business left between us. In the face of death, grieving is our way of coming to terms with all of this, of coming to a place where we neither idealise nor demonise the departed; where we recognise that they both delighted us and irritated us, cracked us up and hacked us off. They were neither a being of pure light nor an agent of darkness.

Sometimes we feel relieved when people die because it ends their pain, or ours. Sometimes the death of someone we loved frees us to discover a strength we never knew we had. In the aftermath of loss, we can feel guilty, angry, clingy, horny… all of this is mourning; all of this is normal.

Mourning allows us to come to terms with a changed world. It's a way of adjusting when the fixtures of life are revealed to be not nearly as fixed as we assumed them to be: when the lover we presumed would always be there no longer is; when the parent who promised to love us forever now loves us only in memory. Mourning transitions us from a world in which the person was, to one in which they are no longer.

It's not just people that die

But it's not just people that die. Sometimes hope dies. Sometimes dreams die. If you watch yourself closely you'll notice that you grieve all kinds of small deaths: a lost job or lost mobility, lost innocence or lost opportunities. We can mourn a broken marriage or losing touch with our kids. Whenever we lose anything we care about we can find ourselves in a place of grief, pining over the loss and wrestling with the pain of letting it go.

Some aspects of our lives are genuinely sad and deserve to be mourned. Maybe our parents didn't understand us quite as much as we would've liked. Maybe they weren't there for us. Maybe we experienced abuse at the hands of someone who claimed to care for us, or maybe those who should have cared failed to protect us. Maybe life has dealt us one cruel blow after another. Maybe we've been rejected, or injured, or made the brunt of ridicule day after day. Mourning gives us the opportunity to face the reality of these situations and come to terms with them. Through mourning we can reach a place where the past remains the past and no longer contaminates the present. Succumbing to our sadness, rather than avoiding it, can be the first step in moving on. Mourning can make us feel better.

The part of us that wants to know God

Of course, some of us prefer to avoid this kind of mourning. We'd rather not feel sad. For some people the evasion of sadness becomes their life's mission. They structure their entire character around not feeling sad, holding themselves above the pain they vaguely sense somewhere inside. They refuse to mourn because mourning hurts and they see no point in being upset over things they can't do anything about. Why add helplessness to the pain they already feel?

Sometimes we carry such intense inner anguish that we fear

we'll collapse entirely if we give in to it. Not only do we refuse to mourn, but we mock the very idea of giving even the slightest ground to the sadness that exposes the real condition of our lives. We ignore it, we exclude it, and commend ourselves for doing so. Instead of befriending our mourning as a channel through which healing can come, we make it an unwelcome guest. We dispatch the vulnerable part of ourselves into exile and believe we've done well.

Perhaps at some early stage of our lives we started off wanting to be loved and accepted, but when this innocent, fragile desire was crushed or rejected or punished, we told ourselves not that this was sad, but that we were wrong to ever expect love or belonging in the first place. We made the desire for affection or acceptance or understanding wrong, so we didn't have to endure the relentless pain of futilely wanting what we could never have. It seemed easier to tell ourselves that the desire was foolish and give it up, than to recognise that we missed something we needed and experience the weakness of mourning its loss.

Sometimes the absence or silence of God in our lives evokes this reaction. We feel we've tried it all before. We tried to meet with God and nothing happened. This sense of spiritual anti-climax can tempt us to collapse, to become dismissive and resigned, to conclude that we were silly to ever think God could be known in the first place.

But if we can bear to remain with our disappointment just for a moment, without judging or rejecting it, we may find we've encountered an often neglected and inconvenient part of ourselves. The part of us that grieves over the silence of God. The part of us that senses his absence and mourns for spiritual connection. If we dare to sit with our disappointment long enough to hear its message we may encounter the part of us that wants to know God.

This disappointment with God shouldn't surprise us. The divines throughout history relate the pain of seeking God and the joy of finding him. The prayers of the mystics are peppered with deep yearning and blissful fulfilment in equal measure. To be disappointed that God hasn't shown up is the beginning of our spiritual journey, not the end of it. If we can stand to mourn, asserts Jesus, we *will* be comforted.

A willingness to mourn therefore opens us to the prospect of receiving comfort. This is why the first beatitude is important. Because without an openness to outside influence our mourning easily gets stuck in itself. Without a window through which comfort can come, we easily despair. To mourn openly is not to indulge ourselves in melancholic fits, but to accept being sad when the need arises, rather than avoiding it – to make no attempt to paint the darker colours out of our emotional spectrum.

When Jesus blesses mourning, therefore, he's blessing those openly saddened in response to something missing from their lives. Our willingness to be sad is a willingness to be attuned to the gains and losses of life. It's a willingness to share the tragic dimension of the human condition. It's also a willingness to receive comfort.

Reprise on an ancient theme

By raising the issue of comfort, Jesus was actually tapping a theme his audience knew well. Throughout the history of the Jewish people, prophetic voices had intermittently arisen. Often during times of crisis, this strange set of men and women were agitated by God to speak into the national conscience. Occasionally heard, but more often ignored, they were the redoubtable individuals who knew what God was up to when everyone else was left guessing. In the years before Christ there was a simple rule in the nation of Israel: if you want to know what God thinks, find yourself a prophet.

Among the most prolific of all the prophets who wrote was Isaiah. He lived seven hundred years before Jesus and, in the latter part of his career, spoke into one of the most turbulent periods of Jewish history. The nation had been invaded by the Babylonian empire and was being deported in several phases to Babylon (present day Iraq) in an attempt by their conquerors to assimilate their culture, to annihilate their identity as a people and erase them from the annals of history.

Isaiah directed several comforting verses into this situation to fortify his countrymen and sustain their hope of a return to their homeland. The comfort he offered wasn't an anaesthetic for their pain, it wasn't a denial of their suffering, nor was it an empty promise. He didn't offer them a comfort blanket or a duvet day. He told them that, in spite of their trauma, God was still with them. He still watched over them and cared for them. He hadn't abandoned them. He still had an eye on them, a vested interest in them, and that when the time was right he would act to save them from their suffering.

It's likely that Jesus evoked these ancient words in the minds of his audience when he spoke of comfort. He spoke to a people again under duress from a foreign power, again beholden to a military machine greater than their own, subjugated this time by Rome rather than Babylon. In the second line of the beatitudes he offered a contemporary reprise on an ancient theme. He conjured up God's promises of the past and cast them into the present.

By blessing the mourners and promising them comfort he was telling an occupied, oppressed people that their sense of loss and bewilderment, their prayers for deliverance, their grief over their predicament, had been heard by God and would be acted upon. At the moment it was first spoken, this beatitude was pertinent, timely and relevant. It hit the nail on the head. And while it had a precise meaning at that time, it also carried a general meaning, a timeless meaning for us now. It publicised God's sympathy for human pain and grief.

Speaking *to* God, not just *about* him

The comfort of the second beatitude therefore rolls down the ages and touches whatever mourning we bring to God today. It commends us for being willing to lay out our stall before God and share our suffering with him in the hope of finding comfort. The beatitude that blesses mourning, blesses us for sharing our deepest needs with God rather than gnawing on them in isolation. We're blessed for speaking *to* God, not just *about* him.

But what does this comfort look like today? What's it like to be comforted by God here-and-now? A few years ago my wife, Marie-Claire, and I took a huge financial risk based on our sense of God's guidance. Having written a cheque that would almost certainly bankrupt us, we lay awake that night terrified that we'd made a terrible mistake. But as we voiced our fears to God in the darkness, a peaceful atmosphere stole into the room and within moments we both knew it would be okay – we could sleep without worry. By the end of that week, we'd received ten thousand pounds to cover the deficit we'd incurred.

When we lay our concerns before God, we never know what will happen next. He may answer instantly, or gradually, or seemingly not at all. Sometimes he answers our prayers in a flash of lightning, at others he seems to be working on geological time, patiently dripping his influence into the world like water on rock. Sometimes the influence of our prayers can only be seen over the long view.

The people Isaiah comforted in exile never saw their homeland again, a whole generation died separated from their native soil in an exile that lasted seventy years. The words of comfort were delivered to sustain them in the waiting, in the anxious time between the promise of return and its fulfilment. The comfort that Isaiah offered his people and which Jesus offers us, lies not so much in the fact that God will answer our prayers instantly, but that he hears us when we pray. The comfort in our mourning is that God draws alongside us and shares our grief. Comfort comes from knowing that whatever bewildering circumstances we may be facing, God is *with* us.

This is, of course, one of the names Isaiah himself applied to Jesus. In an inspired moment of prediction he called the messiah who was to come, *Immanuel*, which translated from Hebrew meant, *God with us*.

The God-we-thought-we-knew

The comfort of God is therefore his presence. He's drawn up a chair alongside our hospital bed. He's hidden himself in our midst and shares our lives in costly attentiveness. The moments we address him needn't find us bored or cowering. Instead, our times with God can be suffused with an atmosphere of deep intimacy as we commune with a loving, intelligent, mysterious power. They can be moments not when our flaws and weaknesses are rudely exposed, but when our deepest desires are voiced and heard. The comfort of God's presence isn't so much that we know him as that he knows us.

But sharing our concerns with God may go against the grain of what we've been taught. The impression of God we've inherited may not be very conducive to voicing what we really think and feel. Maybe we think God doesn't care. If we see him like a Victorian schoolmaster who expects us to stand on ceremony, who'd rather punish than understand, and prefers criticism to curiosity, then stepping into his presence will be like taking a cold-bath in ice-cubes of self-doubting awkwardness. Not the kind of God we'd choose to confide in, more like the colleague we try to avoid sitting next to at the office night out.

Thankfully, Jesus is keen to re-educate us into the notion that God is on our side. He's much more human than we've been led to believe. The great inconsiderate God, who threatened to slay us with a stare, is actually our closest ally in finding our place in the world. The God-we-thought-we-knew silenced us and left us trembling. The God Jesus knows invites us to share our most secret desires and conspires with us to bring them about.

Leave the *how* to God

Another thing that might hinder us seeking comfort from God is our need to know *how* the prayer is going to be answered. What chain of events could possibly bring about the thing we're asking for? It's all very well to claim that God cares, but if he's powerless or too enfeebled to intervene, we'd be better not to waste our breath.

A few years back, a friend of mine found temporary work as a security guard, monitoring the CCTV cameras covering an inner city area. Five nights a week he sat in a tiny room facing a bank of TV screens, watching the streets into the early hours of the morning. If any criminal activity occurred it was his job to catch it on camera. From half a mile away, he'd swivel the lens into position by remote control and zoom in so the police were alerted and hooligans identified. Night after night, week after week, he sat in the dark and watched horrendous acts: a man beaten and kicked to the ground for his wallet, a young woman pressed against a wall and raped, youths fighting to the death with knives. Sometimes the authorities arrived in time to stop the incident, sometimes they didn't. His job was to make sure they had detailed footage of the incident in its entirety. If ever, in a fit of squeamishness, he swung the camera away from an incident, he'd be reprimanded for not doing his job. Sometimes the best he could manage was to focus the picture and close his eyes. After a few months, it broke him – he had a nervous breakdown.

If we view God like a powerless pointer of a distant camera, watching from afar, unable to intervene, we'll never demean ourselves to call on him for help. But if Jesus is to be believed, God isn't a distant monarch watching from a heavenly throne room. He's with us in all of it and able to bring comfort and healing to whatever grieves us.

An example that springs to mind is the time I needed to contact a Ugandan student with urgent information about a visa application, but had no idea how to get hold of him. On my drive home from work a prayer passed my lips before I'd even thought about it. I found myself saying, "Father, I need to see Christopher by the end of the day. Amen."

Straightaway I started to feel stupid. How could God possibly answer it? Shouldn't I have just resigned myself to not being able to reach him in time? I tried to make myself feel better by imagining various ways it could come about: he might send me an email, I could bump into him in the faculty office, he could leave a note on the student notice board. Even if those things happened they wouldn't make any difference. The deadline was the end of the day and we'd run out of time.

I was still thinking about it five minutes later when I got home, only to find Christopher standing outside my house.

This isn't exactly the most dramatic example of answered prayer. It could easily have been a coincidence. But the point I'm making is that sometimes when we pray, it's better to leave the *how* to God. Rather than spend our time second-guessing the mechanics of the response, we make our request and leave it there. If an answer comes, we'll know.

We could therefore say that whenever we become aware of something missing in our lives, a painful desire or a desperate need, we experience a mini-mourning – a sense of loss and a desire to be comforted. As a consequence, we find comfort in God when we share with him what matters most to us and allow him to meet us in it. When we share our inner world with God we give him permission to cross the threshold into our lives with his love. Mourning, in this broader sense of the word, therefore applies to any situation in which we wish to invite God to join us as a sympathetic friend. That's what this experiment is all about.

Whatever seems pertinent

Experiment two therefore involves sharing ourselves with God and looking out for his comfort. It involves talking about how we feel or what bothers us; who we're grateful for or aggrieved at; what confuses or excites us. It's an exercise in spilling out to God whatever's going on, allowing requests to form and offering these as rudimentary prayers.

Here are a few pointers if you'd like to try it.

Experiment 2:

Similarly to the previous experiment, it's probably best to start alone in a comfortable environment. Sitting on a chair or kneeling beside a bed would be good places.

You may like to start with the blessing meditation from the previous experiment to get yourself in a receptive frame of mind, or alternatively just sit still for a few moments, quietening your mind.

If this is one of your first times praying aloud it

may feel a bit strange, so you may want to mark the opening of your prayer time with an invitation to God. Tell him what you're intending to do and invite him to listen to you. There are many different names for God (like Lord or Father) consistent with Jesus' teaching on prayer. So feel free to use whichever comes most naturally to you. Perhaps you could open your prayer time with a statement like, "Lord, I'm going to spend a few minutes talking out my thoughts and concerns to you. I ask that you be here and listen to what I have to say." If you feel silly praying, tell him you feel silly. My own experiments suggest that God is drawn to that kind of honesty.

Then talk to God about anything: your kids, your studies, your marriage, your relationship, your friends, your work, your ambitions, your health, anything at all that's on your mind. The key to sharing yourself with God is to start where you are. No posturing. No airs or graces. No formality. Just take your time and ask yourself, "What really matters to me right now?" And talk out to God whatever seems pertinent. If it helps, imagine him listening and silently nodding in response.

Once you've talked out an issue to God, see if you can find a simple need or request you'd be happy to turn into a single line of prayer. You may want to juggle with the wording until you find a request that works for you, and then state it simply and straightforwardly.

Repeat this process of sharing your thoughts with God and sculpting them into a request as many times as you like, with whatever concerns arise. Maybe just do this once or twice the first time and then extend this as you see fit.

You may want to draw things to a close by thanking God for hearing your prayers. It may sound premature, but it comes from a long spiritual tradition of gratitude to God for having heard our prayers. Saying, "Thank you for listening. Amen" can be a pleasant way to round off our time with God.

A wish sent to the right address

Am I really therefore suggesting that you experiment with making a wish to God? I guess I am. But with a difference. When we throw a coin into a well or blow out the candles on a birthday cake, we rarely know to whom or what we're wishing. We wish blindly to no known address.

Christians over the years have generally been keen to differentiate prayers from wishes. The difference being that when we pray (thanks to Jesus) we now know *who* we are praying to. We're not just putting a message in a bottle and casting it into the ocean, we're directing a postcard to someone we know.

In the end, maybe that's all a prayer is: a wish sent to the right address.

ground

A place to land

Let me give you some advice. If you ever find yourself stranded on open ground in a thunder storm, here's what to do: lie as close to the ground as possible. At least that way, as the lightning streaks across the landscape, it's less likely to choose you as a conductor. Lightning always seeks the path of least resistance to the ground. And, in a sense, so does God. He's always looking for good places to land.

You may have felt that the first two experiments were a bit up in the air, a little bit out there so to speak. Meditating in solitude or voicing our wishes to God could easily be viewed as just taking our imaginations for a stroll. They may be pleasant activities, but they could just be fantasies, pleasurable illusions that make us feel better but make no real difference to the world. This, I guess, is one of the major criticisms of people who seek religious experience, that it so easily becomes an opiate that dulls our senses and detaches us from a genuine responsiveness to real life. It can make us feel better while leaving the world to get worse. This is the peril that faces all would-be disciples: that in seeking God they make themselves irrelevant and useless to the rest of the human race.

If it's any consolation, it seems that Jesus was well aware of this danger. If the beatitudes are anything to go by, he wants us to become real world disciples, not just disembodied mystics. For Jesus it seems, the distinction we might draw between intimacy with God and involvement in the world doesn't exist. So if we love our secret dates with heaven, but worry that they might tempt us to disappear into a blissful numbing fog, then we'll find Jesus on our side. He shares our concern. He's happy for our heads to be in the clouds, so long as our feet remain on the ground.

The experiment I'm offering in this chapter therefore is about grounding our spiritual experience: how we take whatever comfort we've received from God and make it available to the world; how we begin to embody his love; how we become an instrument of his peace; how we offer him a place to land.

So wrong

The third experiment is therefore based on the third beatitude:

> Blessed are the meek,
> for they will inherit the earth.

This, in my experience, is the most well known and most despised of all the beatitudes. Even people who know little about Jesus can be heard quoting this particular line, usually with scorn. Why is it so well known and so generally disliked? Maybe it's because most people view it as naïve, or misguided, or just plain wrong.

I can see why they might think this.

Jesus seems to fly in the face of common sense. By linking meekness with inheritance he appears to be putting together two incompatible variables: a) not asserting ourselves and b) getting what we want. Even simple playground logic knows that meekness and inheritance don't belong together. It tells us that we'll have to fight to get what we want, and that if we choose to be meek (or lack the courage to assert ourselves) we'll have to live with not getting it. In fact, if we choose the way of meekness, it's more likely that other, more demanding people will get whatever it was we'd set our hearts on.

By this logic, choosing to be meek is a crazy choice. It's like choosing to lose. It's a sentiment that doesn't belong in a dog-eat-dog world. Allegedly, it's the ambitious, the self-interested who inherit the earth, not the meek. In a winner-takes-all society, the meek put themselves at a severe disadvantage and the only reason anyone would advocate it as a virtue would be to weaken the competition. Blessed are the meek, for they won't get in our way.

From this angle the notion of the meek inheriting the earth is not only nonsense, but dangerous nonsense. It prevents people grasping opportunities to better themselves. That's why this saying is so well known and so often ridiculed. Because it's viewed as *so* wrong.

Gagging order from God

But for some people, especially those who've had a religious upbringing of the dreary variety, this beatitude can be even more despicable. Not just because it affronts common sense, but because it's been used against them. It's been quoted and re-quoted by authority figures with an interest in ensuring their compliance. For them this beatitude has become an unquestionable gagging order from God, suggesting that everything will be fine if they just shut up – that God rewards silence and passivity in all circumstances.

Some people therefore hate this beatitude because of the context in which it was directed at them. Whenever they spotted unfairness, inequality, abuse or manipulation, they were quickly reminded of the value of meekness in the face of such things. Meekness was reinterpreted to them as silence in the face of injustice, with the promise that putting up with it now would be rewarded one day, somewhere, maybe in heaven.

We need to call this understanding of meekness exactly what it is: spiritual abuse. It falls a long way from Jesus' original intention in blessing the meek.

A free pass to game-players

There is also a further reason why some people turn their noses up at the idea of embracing meekness as a means of inheriting the earth. It strikes them as dishonest. We probably all know people who have developed a way of getting what they want without ever asking for it directly. Instead of making clear requests of other people, they bang crockery loudly round the kitchen, or adopt a helpless and needy appearance, or claim that they don't want the very thing they do want. Some of us learned early in life that we were more likely to get what we wanted if we didn't ask for it. We learned to keep our needs to ourselves. But unfortunately, unbeknown to us, our desires leak out in all kinds of subtle ways that other people can detect. And at times they'll be irritated with us for lacking the gall to ask directly, with all the risk and vulnerability that implies. By not asking for things directly, we expect other people to take the risk of guessing what we're after. We palm off responsibility for ourselves onto other people.

Occasionally this kind of behaviour is badged as meekness or humility, whereas it's more accurately understood as passive-dependence: an unwillingness to reveal what we expect of other people. That's why this beatitude can be viewed as endorsing dishonesty, that Jesus is saying, "Keep it to yourself and what you want will come your way." In other words, he's giving a free pass to game-players, who can appear humble and sweet while getting what they want indirectly by ulterior means, or forcing others to guess. By never asserting themselves they get to look gentle and gracious, but people who know them well find themselves dancing to the tune of all kinds of unsaid needs and expectations. So-called meekness in these situations leaves a sour taste in the mouth because it feels a little bit too much like control, exercised covertly. It's no wonder then, that for many people this beatitude is a hard pill to swallow and one they'd rather leave in its foil wrapper.

Meekness is not weakness

In contradiction to all this though, I'd like to suggest an alternative. In blessing the meek, Jesus issues one of the most profound and freeing statements ever offered to the human race. It isn't designed to forbid us from being ambitious, nor stop us speaking against injustice; nor does it promise us we'll get what we want by hinting. It tells us something much more precious than that. It gives us the single simple condition for being at home and secure in the world. It tells us how to cherish what we have and find satisfaction where we stand. Meekness truly is a beautiful attitude when understood correctly.

So when Jesus blesses the meek and tells them they'll inherit the earth, what exactly is he getting at?

The word "meek" is translated differently by different people. Sometimes it can be read as gentleness. But the overall sense of the blessing is that Jesus is commending people who have a realistic appraisal of themselves and what they're able to achieve in the world; people who therefore aren't tempted into violence or theft or coercion to further their ambitions. Meekness is not weakness, but rather the strength to hold oneself back from insulting or injuring other people, no matter how much we think they might deserve it, and no matter how much we might stand to gain by doing so. The truly meek person respects themselves and other people too much to justify selfish actions by appealing to a favourable outcome. To be meek is to refuse to believe that the end always justifies the means.

I've therefore tended to replace the word meek with the word "grounded". It's not a perfect translation, but it has the advantage of getting us away from some of the more unhelpful misunderstandings of meekness. For most contemporary people, the word meek has an archaic quality that makes it easily misunderstood and irrelevant to modern life. So when I use the word *grounded*, I'm trying to get at the sense of gentleness and presence that meekness implies.

Of course, I'm greatly helped by the fact that the closely related concept of humility is derived from the word *humus*, meaning earth or soil. Humility implies being grounded and I've increasingly noticed that whenever I meet someone who genuinely embodies meekness, I can't help being impressed by the air of quiet confidence that surrounds them, the quality of centredness and presence that characterises them. And consequently I'm happy to talk about learning to be meek as a process of learning to know our limits, of learning to keep our feet on the floor, or learning to be grounded.

Being grounded in the way that I'm using the term means a willingness to centre our attention on the immediate concerns of the here-and-now; of realising that if there is a bigger battle to be fought, or a larger purpose to be pursued, it can only be moved towards in the present moment and nowhere else. Being grounded means being present right now, no matter how mundane it may be; being aware that we cannot skip over ordinary time like a less favoured track on an otherwise excellent CD, because it's the anvil on which our extraordinary times are being forged.

If we absent ourselves from normal life, seeing it as beneath us, we may hamper our ability to savour the taste of pleasure and success when they do come. Being grounded means a willingness to embrace whatever interruption, distraction or frustration blocks our way as an integral and inevitable part of the winding course of life – not seeing people or problems as obstacles to be eliminated in building a through-road to success. Being grounded means, as much as possible, keeping our centre of gravity within ourselves. It means acting out of an inner sense and wisdom rather than seeing our value in the pursuit of whatever attracts us.

Only here can we love

Nevertheless, this kind of groundedness, attractive though it is, isn't always easy. Being relatively ambitious, I have a tendency to identify the things I want to achieve and go after them for all I'm worth. And while this can bring energy and excitement to living, it does mean that I sometimes find the slower more pedestrian aspects of life difficult to appreciate. When I'm at my most industrious, the goal becomes everything and I easily become fixated on it to the exclusion of friends, colleagues and family. My self-worth somehow gets attached to the achievement of some relatively minor activity and suddenly the whole reason for my existence hinges on my next lecture or project. I become allergic to the present moment – reality intolerant. I end up living in a future that hasn't arrived yet and ignoring the challenges and consolations of the moment.

When I wrote about mourning in the previous chapter, I said that we can mourn over the state of our marriage, or losing touch with our kids. For me this is a good example of where one beatitude slowly phases into the next. Because for me the sadness that hits me when I realise that I've been at home in body but not in mind, that I've been physically present but psychologically absent, is profoundly moving. When I open my eyes and see a family that needs my attention while I've been off in my imagination delivering lectures to a non-existent audience, I'm suddenly confronted with the great sadness of missing a stretch of time. I'm faced with the fact that I'm squandering never-to-be-repeated instants with the most precious people in my life and that there may come a time when it's too late to make up for all the moments I've turned away from playing marbles with my boys, or arranging a date with my wife. To be meek or grounded, is to no longer take offence at the ordinariness of everyday life and thereby flee the present moment, but rather to refuse to miss out on unique, unrepeatable moments of connection by being in the here-and-now. Only here can we love; only now can we be loved.

The right to be here

When Jesus promised the meek that they would inherit the earth, it could be that he had some future date in mind, when paradise has arrived and the earth is renewed and those who benefit most will be characterised by this quality he calls meekness. But there could be another more immediate meaning than that. Could it be that his blessing has a dose of common sense genius to it? That it's only by being meek and grounded that we can possibly possess each moment we live in? That only by being centred in real time, can we possibly inherit as a gift the patch of ground we currently stand on and inhabit the moment we pass through?

Jesus didn't say the meek would rule the world, he said they'd inherit the earth. It's a subtle but significant difference.

When people laugh at this beatitude it's because they assume he's saying the meek will gain the world. That a bunch of lowly, ordinary, clueless people are somehow destined to ascend to the positions of prestige and power that govern our world. That the insignificant are destined for global domination. As a promise this isn't necessarily impossible, but it's pretty unlikely and hence laughable.

But Jesus doesn't say that. He says the meek are blessed because they will inherit the earth. In other words there's a quality of existence that can't be gained by raw ambition alone, but only through groundedness: the feeling that we have the right to be here. Not just that we've risen to prominence by hook or by crook, through affiliation or the services of a good publicist, but that we can stand securely as legitimate possessors of our own lives.

Being well grounded is therefore not antagonistic to ambition. Being gentle or humble doesn't prevent us from being aspirational or relentless in directing our lives. Taking ground gradually is sometimes the surest and most reliable way to make progress, like when a rising tide claims the beach. The waves can lap in so slowly that we fail to notice the shoreline gradually shrinking until we're up to our ankles. Being grounded means enjoying each step in the journey, enjoying what we have and not being prepared to trade it in for a bit more. The meek inherit the earth not because they grab at what they lack, but because they value and enjoy what they have.

Whenever I meet or hear about highly successful people, I'm often curious about whether they've managed to remain grounded, at home in themselves, in their rise to celebrity. Those who mange to remain grounded seem to carry fame and success effortlessly. They know how to enjoy it, they seem grateful for it, and seem to accept that it may not last and should be treasured while it does. But I'm equally struck by the extreme restlessness that seems to afflict people who reach the top of their game, but never seem to settle in it. They dip in and out of the limelight, staging frequent comebacks, never able to relax, constantly fearing that their power or influence will be stripped from them. They seem terrified that they're missing out on something, not doing as well as they could be, or somehow falling short. They gain the world, it seems, but lose their identity. Without being grounded they lack the ease required to carry greatness with gratitude.

Thankfully, if we rewind a couple of thousand years back to Jesus on the mountainside, we realise that in blessing the meek he was tackling precisely this kind of concern. It seems that he had a prophetic inkling that the society he was addressing was about to come to an abrupt and violent end, and was therefore well aware that anyone with political aspirations to climb the ladder of power would share the same fate as their doomed nation.

Forty years later (in AD70) the Romans demolished the temple in Jerusalem and ended the Jewish nation in its first-century form. Jesus in his teaching had warned his followers of the crisis to come and advised them of the signs to flee the city and escape. So when he blessed the meek, the ordinary, the grounded, the modest and level-headed, he was implying that it wasn't ultimately the politically savvy who'd come out on top, but rather those humble enough to heed a warning and unencumbered enough to run, who'd live to see another day. Those with listening ears and light feet would wake up next morning alive with the ones they loved.

Meekness doesn't oppose ambition, but it does teach us to be wary of it – to enjoy our fleeting successes and stay grounded no matter how high we soar. At least that way, when we do fall, the fall will never be too far.

Decide to be present

The third experiment will therefore be fairly familiar to anyone who's practiced sensory awareness exercises or learned mindfulness techniques. It involves being grounded, aware and non-judgemental of the present moment, so that we can be and act effectively within it.

It isn't particularly *Goddy* – by which I mean it doesn't necessarily involve addressing or contemplating God as the previous experiments have done. It wouldn't surprise me though if you find practicing it a profoundly spiritual experience. Whenever we locate ourselves mindfully in the present moment God can use it as an opportunity to find us. In fact, it could be said that the immediate moment is the only place we can possibly meet God. Not only that, but it's only in the here-and-now that transformation can take place, in ourselves and in the world at large. So although this experiment doesn't explicitly mention God, it doesn't mean he's absent from it. In fact, we shouldn't be taken aback if we run into him the moment we decide to ground ourselves.

It's been suggested that this is the kind of awareness Jesus practiced all the time. That he was constantly engaged and present, and that this accounts for his incredible responsiveness to the people he met. It explains his spontaneity in the situations he encountered. Perhaps groundedness was the secret of his constant connection with God, the wiring of his live-link with heaven? Maybe it could be the same for us.

So here's the experiment:

Experiment 3:

This experiment can be done anywhere, but it's often best performed during routine activities like preparing food, washing up, walking to work, or any other time we're likely to find ourselves avoiding the present moment by thinking about other things. You can even be halfway through something and decide to start the experiment.

Start by choosing to remain in the present moment as much as you possibly can. Instead of allowing your mind to wander, you're going to attend to your current experience of whatever you're doing.

Pay particular attention to your five senses. If you're peeling vegetables, look at the colours, feel the textures, smell the fragrances of what you're doing. If taking a walk, look at what's around you, feel your feet as they touch the ground with each step, pay attention to what you can hear. If sitting still, notice the weight of your body on the chair, the warmth of your feet, the sound of your breath. Whatever you're doing, decide to be present and attentive to the here-and-now, even in stressful situations.

Try to suspend judgements you might make about the world you experience, try to allow it just to be and observe without judging. Bring your awareness to your current experience of the world. If you do find you're distracted or drawn away into daydreaming, don't judge this, just notice it and draw your attention gently back to present experience.

If, after doing this for a few minutes, you feel as if you'd like to extend the exercise further, you can experiment with adopting a prayerful gratitude towards the world around you. Not praying with words, but simply beaming out a sense of thankfulness for this tree, or that food, or these children, or the chair, or whatever it is that holds your attention.

It could be that as you do this you encounter situations that require action or intervention. If so, ask yourself what the most gracious, effective or skilful way to meet this demand would be. These are the moments when gentleness allows us to be effective, the moments when meekness inherits the earth.

Being awake and being present

This exercise has been with me since my first year at university. I first read it one morning before a psychology lecture. It was a half-hour walk to campus, so I practiced this new state of consciousness all the way to university: feeling my feet touching the ground, noticing the breeze on my forehead, attending to the warmth of the paving stones and the green shoots of grass that grew between them. I felt the movement of my limbs, the rhythm of my breathing. For once, I suspended my usual mad dash that turned the journey to work into a long grey corridor and suddenly the world around me sprang into living colour. I actually *saw* the people I passed and wondered about their lives. Psychologists would call this uptime, or sensory awareness, or mindfulness. The name doesn't really matter, to me it just felt like being awake and being present.

Unfortunately, on that occasion I so enjoyed the stroll that I was late for class and arrived to a lecture theatre packed with hundreds of students. I was forced to sit conspicuously on the steps of the aisle instead of in the audience. The title of the talk was, "How to become a clinical psychologist" and I was there because that's what I wanted to be. In the end that's exactly what I became – a clinical psychologist. But to this day I still can't remember anything that was said in the lecture. The walk there, however, has remained vibrant in my mind ever since.

sort

Ctrl-alt-del moments

I once heard a story about a computer science teacher who was asked to take over a class at short notice. One of his colleagues was off sick and he was the replacement. But he didn't know what he was doing and didn't have time to get to grips with what he was about to teach. So when he stood in the lecture theatre in front of a hundred scribbling students, nerves got the better of him and his mind went blank.

This happened a few times. It was always the same. He'd be facing the whiteboard, halfway through a word, and lose track of what he was writing. He'd stand there, frozen with his back to the class, hand in the air poised to write, mind entirely absent. It only ever lasted a few seconds, but it felt like eons.

After a while the class wised up to what was going on and the next time it happened, a note was passed along the benches. It read: "Your lecturer has crashed. Please press ctrl-alt-del to restart."

The more I've thought about that story, the more it's become a sort of parable for me of the hiatus moments in life. The moments when we crash. I call them ctrl-alt-del moments.

They're the times when it dawns on us that we can't go on the way we've been going. We become aware that the rules we've used to organise our lives so far don't serve us quite as well as they used to and the cracks are starting to show. Our operating system needs an upgrade.

Ctrl-alt-del moments often accompany times of transition: moving house or leaving home, making wedding vows or filing divorce papers, having children or grandchildren, being promoted or getting the sack. Situations like these not only confront us with a constantly changing world, but also with the fact that we too will have to change and adapt if we're going to survive our new circumstances.

And it hurts. It's painful to see our most cherished expectations and rules of thumb flounder in uncharted seas. It torments us to see well established habits or faithful sayings on trial. That's what midlife crises are made of.

But if we have the eyes to see it, we may notice that ctrl-alt-del moments, painful though they are, can also be fantastic opportunities. They not only require us to change, they allow us to grow. They may send a fault-line through the structure of our lives, but they also give us a chance to rebuild ourselves differently. Our failures can liberate us. Our uncertainties can sprout possibilities. Tragedy can embolden us. Bewilderment can ennoble us.

Being shaken up like this can also lead to intense spiritual development. It can push us to seek a purpose deeper than the spinning kaleidoscope of our daily concerns. Nothing sends us skidding into the God Lab faster than a ctrl-alt-del moment.

Chastity belts and temperance movements

Our first three experiments looked at attitudes that are highly relevant to times of transition. They looked at being open, sharing and grounded. We need all three if we're going to navigate the chaos evoked by change. Openness allows us to discover that wonderful opportunities may be found in every disruption. Sharing our concerns with God lets us mourn the loss of the old order, so we free ourselves to offer a clean slate for the new. Groundedness prevents us escaping into avoidance or illusion by training our eyes on the here-and-now, awaiting the future that comes next. These attitudes are our friends if we intend to grow through times of change.

But what does this kind of growth look like? It's all very well knowing that transition lends us an opportunity to revise our way of life, but what kind of life should we move towards? If ctrl-alt-del moments can free us *from* an old way of being, what are we freed *to*? This is what our fourth experiment addresses. And as ever, it's based on the fourth beatitude spoken by Jesus in the fifth chapter of Matthew's gospel:

> Blessed are those who hunger and thirst for righteousness,
>   for they will be satisfied.

A few years ago, I was asked to speak in church on this verse and happened to mention it to a friend at work. When I told him I was speaking about *blessed are those who hunger and thirst for righteousness*, he was quick to say that it sounded pretty uninspiring. This confused me because I was quite excited about speaking on it. I suggested it became more inspirational the better we understood it. He said, "Oh." And the conversation ended there.

Righteousness it seems, like meekness, has a bad rep.

Part of the reason for this is that, in English at least, righteousness is an old word that for most people belongs to a bygone era. Like chastity belts and temperance movements it belongs with the Victorians perhaps, or maybe even the Puritans. For most people it evokes images of austerity, dark suits and sombre expressions. It's not an appealing image. It's the opposite of fun. It's definitely not something we'd want to hunger and thirst after.

I'm sure this was the image of righteousness my colleague had in mind when he dismissed it as uninspiring. I'm equally sure that he didn't want to talk about it any further for fear of having his own lifestyle put under the spotlight. If starchy sobriety was the only alternative, he'd rather have his life as it was: perhaps broken and painful at times, but at least free from the straight-jacket of having to pretend to be good. If anything were to draw him towards a different life, it would have to be something better than this vacuous caricature of righteousness.

Hate people in the name of love

Righteousness is also often confused with *self*-righteousness – the strategy of increasing our self-worth by claiming to be morally better than other people. Self-righteousness is a way of elevating ourselves above the herd by preening our ethical feathers and taking pride in our moral standing – sometimes even believing that God likes us better than anyone else.

Self-righteousness is, therefore, inherently hypocritical because it protests its goodness, rightness and humility while diminishing the moral value of others. It presents itself as compassion while fuelling itself through contempt. It prides itself on giving, while subtly taking. Self-righteousness is moral vampirism. It survives by sucking the life-blood out of others, because it needs other people to fail and fall to keep the upper hand. Like a white-washed tomb, it's dazzling on the outside, but living death within. I know, I've lived it.

To be fair, I suspect all human beings are hypocrites to some extent. We all, at some point, even without knowing it, present ourselves as something we're not. We all play-act at times. We're all prone to self-deception and operate in bad faith. But to my mind, self-righteousness is a particularly obnoxious form of hypocrisy, given its tendency to hate people in the name of love.

One of the least attractive features of self-righteousness is the great delight it takes in being right – and harshly imposing this rightness on other people, even in small things. It reminds me of a friend of mine who was brought up by a very strict Great Aunt. One Summer, as a young girl of nine or ten, she decided to go down the road to buy an ice-cream from the corner shop. On her way out, she took her raincoat off the peg by the door (just in case). Her Great Aunt, watching her, immediately wanted to know why she would be so stupid as to take a raincoat down the road on a summer's day. My friend responded that it just might rain and therefore she was taking it (just in case). She was told in no uncertain terms that it wouldn't rain and she should do without it.

Deciding that the fight wasn't worth it, my friend as a little girl left her raincoat on the hook, and went down the road in her shirt sleeves. But in the five minute walk from home to the corner shop, the heavens opened and soaked her to the skin. When she came home drenched her Great Aunt had nothing to say. My friend stomped up to her room speechless with rage.

And for some people, that's been their experience of righteousness – the unreasoning assertion of rightness, bulldozing through whatever seemed prudent or wise to them. Fair enough, sometimes people do know better than we do, and at such times we do well to listen. But at other times they get a kick out of *thinking* they know better than we do and this is what's so objectionable in self-righteousness.

Righteousness really does have a bad rep. And it's therefore no surprise that it hardly inspires people. Like a lot of religious language, our understanding of righteousness has been contaminated. The pure water offered to us by Jesus has been ruined and poisoned, so we grimace at the thought of drinking it.

But if Jesus is correct in blessing us for wanting righteousness at all costs, if he's right in suggesting that this yearning will yield satisfaction for us, then righteousness simply can't mean what we've been led to believe it means. It can't be hypocrisy, or living death, or fanatical rightness. Righteousness must be something else.

But what?

More concerned with looking good than being good

The contamination of our understanding of righteousness isn't just a recent phenomenon. It was also a big issue in Jesus' day. The religious leaders of his time weren't all bad, but if his critique of them is accurate, they tended to be more self-righteous than righteous.

To be fair to them, they were only behaving like many religious people do when the practice of their faith is under threat. They self-consciously performed religious duties like praying, fasting and giving to the poor as a way of distinguishing themselves from the paganism of their Roman invaders. They were marking their territory and asserting their identity in a hostile environment. Unfortunately, in the process, they became more preoccupied with looking good than being good; more concerned with impressing people than meeting God.

So when Jesus blesses those who hunger and thirst for righteousness, he's commending people with a heartfelt desire for it – those who see through the religious veneer and find it wanting; those who tire of play-acted goodness and want to pursue an authentic ethical existence. He's blessing those who know that being good in and of itself is its own reward, irrespective of whether it looks good to other people.

Jesus was probably speaking Aramaic when he blessed the crowd like this. He was speaking the language appropriate to their time and place. But in English we can't deny that right-eous is a word that's largely fallen into disuse. In the past it was often rendered right*wise*ness. It was a relative term, concerned with how we related to ourselves, to other people and God. It was more to do with right relationships than right opinions. To live right*wise* was to live a good life, a life well-aligned and oriented to the task of living; a life governed by wisdom; a life that was praiseworthy, consistent and deserving of respect.

Righteousness, therefore, in its original rendering, far from being oppressive or unattractive, sums up the highest aspira-tions of being human. To hunger and thirst for righteousness is to want, above all else. to become the people we're meant to be; to outgrow childish squabbling and petty concerns, to fulfil our potential for goodness, to live in the full weightiness of our decisions and respect ourselves for doing so. Thirsting for righteousness isn't just a concern for our own piety, it means wanting the best not just for ourselves but for everyone we know. To hunger and thirst for righteousness is the desire to see goodness and justice proliferate in the world, starting with us.

A fragment of slang

I once asked a group of students to come up with a synonym for the word righteousness. We'd talked about some of the confusion that occurs around the word and thought about what it might really mean. They then took some time in groups to consider which word could best replace righteous, if they were attempting to explain it in a conversation over the kitchen table.

The first few suggestions were obvious. One group came up with the word *nice.* But we thought better of that pretty quickly. Nice seemed too fluffy, too inoffensive even. Not that we were opposed to courtesy or good manners, but niceness didn't capture some of the strength in righteousness. It didn't get at the moral courage that righteous people often embody. Niceness is easily confused with mere compliance or acquiescence or flattery, whereas righteousness galvanises people to stand out from the crowd if needed. Righteousness has backbone, it's not always nice.

The next suggestion was *good*. Maybe we could talk about someone being good, instead of righteous. We were getting warmer. The word good has the same richness and strength as righteousness. It can encompass lots of things: ethical purity, consistency, soundness, wellbeing – most of the stuff that righteousness gets at. Good is a good word. But we still weren't quite satisfied. It's a good word, but maybe too good. Maybe it means too many things? There's no real agreement in our culture about what a "good life" looks like. Do we mean a pleasurable life? A meaningful life? An ethical life? All three maybe? As far as a conversation over coffee was concerned, goodness wouldn't help us much, because it left us still having to define exactly what we meant by it. It left us in the same conundrum we had with righteousness, having to explain exactly what we meant so as not to be misunderstood. For our purposes, good was not good enough.

And then the third suggestion was, well, weird!

The third candidate to replace righteousness in everyday conversation was *sorted*. Just in case you're not familiar with this particular example of colloquial English, when we say that someone is sorted, we mean they know where it's at. They look life in the eye with understanding and know what to do with it. They know how to live. It's sort of the opposite of screwed up. It means someone's sorted their life out, has balance, poise and presence. They garner our respect because they're trustworthy, they have integrity. We can count on them to do what they think is right, even when it costs, and not conform just for the sake of popularity. When we say someone's *sorted* we're saying we like them and admire them, and to some extent aspire to imitate them.

It seemed an unusual move to replace the elegant historic English of *righteousness* with a fragment of slang. But the more I've thought about it, the more appropriate I think the replacement is. It might not be so unusual to think that when Jesus blesses those who hunger and thirst for righteousness, he's commending us for wanting to sort our lives out. He's blessing us for wanting to be sorted and, by implication, reassuring us when we know we're not. Insofar as righteousness means an ironing out, an ordering of our relationships, a restoration of our connectedness, a composure in our approach to life, then sorted strikes me as a fairly decent label for a pretty cool way of being.

Being more myself

I think I find the notion of hungering and thirsting for righteousness exciting because it's very close to the bone for me. For most of my adult life I've found myself returning to a simple prayer. Every now and then I turn my attention to God and say, "Father, please do with me whatever you need to do, to make me into the person you need me to be."

When I see it in black and white like that, it strikes me for the first time as a potentially masochistic prayer. A prayer that God will "use" me could be viewed as a plea submitted to a tyrant. If I'm asking God to use me, am I not also giving him free reign to *ab*use me? But it's never occurred to me like that when I've prayed it. I've always viewed it as quite an exciting prayer to pray.

I find it exciting because ultimately I trust the God that Jesus represents. I trust that if I put myself at his disposal with a prayer like this, his intentions towards me are good. He won't send me jumping through hoops just for the fun of it. He doesn't want a dancing slave, he wants a willing apprentice, ready to be put through his paces in learning to live.

Furthermore, over time I've formed the impression that God has a better sense of who I am and what I'm to become than I have myself. So when I ask him to make me into who he needs me to be, I'm not asking to be scarred and mutilated into a diminished version of myself, but yearning to become who I'm meant to be. I'm asking him to grow the tiny seed of my potential, to fan into flame the glowing embers within me. To put it vaguely, I have a sense that somehow in some way something in me is up to something big (something in us all perhaps). And when I ask God to make me the person he needs me to be, I'm giving him permission to do whatever needs to be done to allow this better version of myself to emerge.

More often than not, I catch myself praying this prayer when I'm dissatisfied with myself, during those ctrl-alt-del moments when I hit the wall, or run into a roadblock, or draw a dead-end; the moments when I don't know what to do with what's in front of me, or what to do with myself; the times when I face yet another opportunity to learn, another chance to sort myself out. It's dissatisfaction with the way I'm dealing with things that leaves me longing to be sorted.

But the strange thing is this. Every time this prayer is answered and I take a small but significant step towards being a bit more sorted, a bit wiser, a little more artful in playing the game of life, it doesn't feel alien or different, but as somehow being more like myself. It doesn't feel like a foreign-body bolted on to my life. It feels a bit like coming home. In praying that God would make me the person he needs me to be, I find myself becoming more fully the person I am. In asking to be more like him, I change to become more like me.

And this is what Jesus promises when we hunger and thirst for righteousness. He says we'll be satisfied. We'll get what we've asked for. We'll feel that the deficit has been filled. In fact, I'd even go as far as to say that the desire to be righteous, the drive to be sorted, is one of the few human needs that can always be satisfied no matter what our circumstances may be. So long as we have the capacity to decide we can always deal with our circumstances better. We can always seek to find a wiser response to our daily challenges. We can always find some growth for ourselves in the difficulties that come our way. We can answer the questions that life throws at us by becoming more of who we're meant to be. We may not always get what we want, but we can choose how we respond and therefore who we become as a result. Blessed are those who want to be sorted, for they will be satisfied.

A chance to befriend us

The experiment attached to this beatitude, therefore, is a good old-fashioned exercise in confession. But don't let that put you off. It doesn't involve confessional booths or rosary beads or a solemn word in the vestry. It's a bit more stripped down than that. But it still may not be the most appealing experiment for some people.

We may flinch at the thought of confession because it involves admitting we've done something wrong and we're usually pretty reluctant to do that. Certainly for me, if I resist the idea of *confessing my sins* it's because I'd rather not admit I made a mistake. I'd rather think that I did the best I could with the situation I found myself in, given my understanding at the time. I'd rather view it as my best effort (which it was) rather than out-and-out wrongness. Besides, the idea of saying sorry to God sometimes seems a bit childish to me. It's more like the kind of patter I offered Mrs Pensie at the age of seven when I had to apologise for disturbing her sleep by playing the bugle outside at six in the morning (I haven't done that since by the way). Somehow it's not quite the way an adult takes responsibility for their errors.

But this is a caricature of confession. It's actually much more than just a quick apology for wrongdoing. It's not God's chance to humiliate us or rub our noses in it. Confession gives God a chance to befriend us. It gives him a chance to accept us and meet us in the areas of our lives we'd rather gloss over. Confession is one of the practical ways we can invite God to get involved in the process of becoming who we're meant to be. It's connecting rather than being told off. It's a gentle way of seeking to be sorted.

Confession assumes that we never quite reach the pinnacle of our potential and sometimes we fall very short of it. We fall short not just in individual actions, like cheating on taxes, losing tempers or spurning spouses, but in that many of our short-comings are habitual. They're entrenched patterns in our psycho-logical make-up. They're our *modus operandi* in dealing with the world.

We confess, therefore, not just our actions, but our recurrent tendencies: our foibles, addictions and weaknesses. We confess that not only do we not know how to stop them, but we also may not want to. We may not be able to imagine life without them.

The human condition therefore hangs somewhere between the shining lights of heaven and the dust of the earth. Confession is a way of bridging the gap, accepting ourselves as we are while siding with who we're to become. It's a way of pursuing godliness without ignoring our humanity. It's a practical way of hunger-ing and thirsting for righteousness.

We'll therefore finish with the experiment, as follows:

Experiment 4:

Find ten or fifteen minutes to be alone and identify some area of your life where you are dissatisfied with yourself – somewhere you feel you let yourself down or don't do as well as you should; an area where you don't live up to being the person you think you should be. It could be anything.

Think for a moment and invite God to join you in the thinking. Allow yourself to imagine what you would be like if you outgrew or improved this problematic tendency in life. Who would you have to be for this pattern of behaviour to disappear? Get a clear picture of what this better version of yourself would look like.

If you dare, offer a prayer to God, inviting Him to get involved in bringing about this better self. Ask Him to do whatever needs to be done in your life to make you the person you're meant to be. You may even want to use my prayer: Father, do whatever you need to do, to make me the person you need me to be.

You may then want to confess to God that this unsatisfactory pattern or tendency in you falls short of who you're meant to be, and doesn't belong to the person you're becoming. The word sin originally meant "missing the mark". To confess is to acknowledge that you're missing the mark.

Having confessed, notice any changes in how you feel in your body. Before closing the experiment, spend a few moments enjoying the idea that God has met you – that you've been accepted as you are and that he's working with you to become the person you're meant to be.

free

Caught in the crossfire

In the fourth beatitude, as we just saw, Jesus blesses those who want righteousness. He roots for those who want to see the world put right and themselves sorted out. In the fifth beatitude, as we're about to see, he follows this with a blessing on those who are merciful. It's the next marker on our spiritual journey and it reads like this:

> Blessed are the merciful,
> for they will receive mercy.

At first glance we might think that these two blessings contradict one another. Our previous experiment was all about wanting ourselves and the world to be put right. It implied that there's something wrong with us and the world that needs to be corrected.

But this one is all about mercy. Jesus is cheerleading those who can live graciously in a world that's less than ideal. He's celebrating the patience needed to live in a world that often doesn't change for the better. On the one hand he blesses us for wanting to be sorted and on the other he blesses us for being able to live with the fact that we're not. Which does he want from us, a determination to change things or a willingness to tolerate the way things are?

It's like wandering up to a signpost at a crossroads. In one direction it reads: change the world. In the other: accept the world. We can't go both ways at the same time. Surely we can't change the world by accepting it? It's a contradiction. We're caught in the crossfire between two incompatible principles.

Tripping over mercy

But sometimes being caught in the crossfire is a good place to be. We're never more alive than when attempting to weave together apparently opposing ideas.

It goes without saying that if righteousness is a life lived rightly (a sorted life) then a merciful attitude towards others has to be part of that kind of living. One of the dangers of any kind of spiritual growth is that we start to think we're a step ahead of other less enlightened individuals. We look down on anyone who hasn't got it, who hasn't been initiated or liberated.

But true righteousness, true sortedness, true growth, doesn't draw distinctions like this. It doesn't need to. It enjoys being what it is and happily shares this with other people. In fact, any so-called righteousness that leaves us snobby about the spiritual credentials of our peers is suspect. It's more like an ego trip than a spiritual journey.

So, if we pursue righteousness – a better self, a better world – we sooner or later run into the need for mercy. We'll need it for other people because they'll fail to meet our standards. We'll need it for ourselves, because we'll fail to meet them too.

This is just another example of one beatitude leading us to the next. The desire to be righteous takes us only so far before we find ourselves tripping over mercy.

A well known phone number

Over years of being in church, of reading and listening to sermons, I've accumulated a lot of received wisdom. Quite often I don't know who came up with it or where the ideas originated, but they quickly become part of my folk theology. This is the backdrop of ideas against which I make sense of what it means to follow Jesus.

One thing I've noticed is that mercy is often mentioned in the same breath as grace. Grace and mercy are a kind of biblical double-act, as inseparable as Laurel and Hardy. They occur together in my mind. They trip off my tongue in a single breath like a well known phone number.

Yet, while they seem to belong together they're often contrasted when formally defined. Almost as if someone felt the need to offer us a few pointers on telling identical twins apart. They often turn up together. They look pretty similar, even identical to the untrained eye, so we need a few distinguishing features just in case we meet one of them alone and need to get their name right.

An illustration might help at this point.

Let's say (hypothetically, of course) that my wife has just had a birthday and received as a present the most delicious box of Swiss chocolates ever to pass the threshold of our home. And let's say (hypothetically, of course) that some kind of loose agreement was made between her and I that the chocolates were hers and that it would be high treason on my part to consume any of them without her permission. And let's also say (still hypothetically) that one evening, feeling suddenly peckish, I conclude that only her scrumptious Swiss truffles could possibly fill the hole in my stomach. And therefore breaking our unwritten confectionery pact, I start unwrapping one of those sumptuous golden packages. And let's just say (hypothetically remember) that at that very instant my wife enters the room to discover me not involved with another woman, but much worse: involved with another chocolate.

This trivial (not to mention hypothetical) example, illustrates the kind of situation to which mercy applies. We catch someone red-handed, undeniably and inexcusably in the wrong.

Justice or fairness demands recompense. Perhaps a demonstration of remorse or some kind of repayment. In this case, replacement of the pilfered chocolate with something of equal value.

Mercy, on the other hand, while still recognising that I was caught red-handed in breach of our agreement, absorbs the burden of the crime. Mercy frees me. It responds by letting me off the hook.

Grace, according to it's popular definition, not only lets me off, but perhaps invites me to enjoy the rest of the chocolate box. Whereas mercy holds back from giving the deserved punishment, grace goes further. It gives us a gift. In this case I receive as a gift the very chocolates I would have stolen.

These definitions tell us when we can show mercy. We need mercy for people who've done us wrong. We can only let someone off the hook if we've had them dangling from a hook in the first place.

And when Jesus eyeballed the crowd and blessed the merciful, he wasn't asking a team of office staff to put up with the guy who always jammed the photocopier. He was addressing an occupied and brutalised ethnic group, and strengthening the resolve of those who refused to give themselves over to justifiable hatred. Mercy is a response to something wrong. It means not plotting to punish people as we think they deserve.

Mercy isn't passive

But if we're not careful with these definitions we start thinking that mercy is a passive attitude – that it involves *not* doing something.

But grace and mercy overlap. They're like a couple who finish each other's sentences. It's sometimes difficult to know where mercy ends and grace begins. Mercy as Jesus views it isn't a negative movement, or a negation, or an absence. If we think that mercy means doing nothing we're likely to fall for its impostors. We'll be fooled by those attitudes and actions that call themselves mercy but don't really deserve it.

Sometimes, for example, we'd very much like to punish someone or take revenge on them, but for some reason can't. Maybe they're more powerful than we are, or maybe there was no opportunity, or maybe we're too scared, or maybe we fear to damage our reputation. Whatever the reason, we withhold retaliation but continue to carry the intention to harm them. Superficially it looks like mercy, but it's actually a grudge. We can even look kind to their face, but mercilessly assassinate their character behind closed doors. We may convince ourselves that this is mercy, but it's not. It's more like playacting.

There's also another impostor of mercy. It would have been familiar to Jesus' audience, or anyone else who has to deal with authority figures who control people through fear. It's a favoured strategy among dictators and godfathers. Sometimes we encounter it in political scuffles in the workplace, when someone more senior than ourselves forgives us for an embarrassing error, or helps us out of a mess of our own making with apparent magnanimity. Having helped us they assume they own us. There are strings attached. They've done us a favour or overlooked our failure, but now we owe them. Their "mercy" was a down payment on our future loyalty. And behind it all lies the threat that if we let them down again or forget their generosity, things will get really nasty. It's not mercy, just punishment postponed – a suspended sentence. It looks like mercy but it's actually a subtle form of control based on a sense of obligation.

Mercy isn't just a lapse into silence nor a menacing suspension of punishment. True mercy requires energy, generosity and determination. Extending mercy to people who've wronged us requires resourcefulness on our part.

We sometimes refer to truly merciful people as *big*. Those who are kind enough to give us the benefit of the doubt when news of our mistakes reaches their ears. Those who choose to believe the best of us rather than swallow whole the latest gossip. We know they didn't have to do it. We think it's big of them when they let us off the hook and give us a chance.

The mercy that Jesus recommends isn't passive, it requires us to be *big*. It isn't just the absence of a chance to retaliate, it's largesse and strength of character. If we're to be merciful we'll need to give of ourselves, sometimes painfully.

A verbal hand grenade

This is one of the reasons why mercy is so difficult to practice. It has a reverse logic to it. It means not treating people as we think they deserve. So, in a sense, we need mercy to deal with precisely those people and situations we don't think deserve mercy.

Mercy applies when we want justice, we want recompense, we want vengeance, we want some kind of arbitration, someone to come and sort things out. Mercy applies to all those situations where we're inclined to shout foul or demand intervention from a heavenly referee. It applies to those moments when we say, "If there was a God, this kind of thing wouldn't happen." This is why mercy is so difficult to think about, because it's the opposite of the response we'd like to make. When Jesus blesses the merciful he surely can't be saying that we should be merciful at all times in all places? We can't forgive everything!

Jesus speaks mercy into a world that isn't always fair, no matter how much we demand it should be. And the crowd he spoke to knew that unfairness first hand. Under military occupation, they'd witnessed torture and brutality, if not to themselves then to people they knew; under the heel of an oppressive regime that didn't flinch from public execution as a deterrent to potential uprising. Jesus himself was crucified as only one among thousands of such examples. Just another naked man, dispatched in agony on a cross. Another warning from Imperial Rome to its occupied territories: don't get above yourself; know your place. This is what happens to would-be reformers.

Not surprisingly, therefore, Israel in Jesus' era was a hotbed of revolutionary fervour. Various factions plotted the violent overthrow of Roman rule. They weren't going to go quietly. They weren't going to know their place. They wanted justice. They wanted payback and most importantly they wanted the freedom to govern themselves as a nation.

In speaking up for mercy, Jesus was lobbing a verbal hand grenade into an inflammatory situation. To people, some of whom harboured justifiable intentions for vengeance and uprising, he endorsed mercy. It was an inappropriate time to voice such thoughts, offensive to even float the idea of letting their Roman masters off the hook – unthinkable, even. Mercy could come later maybe. After the uprising. After the victory. After freedom was regained. Mercy could prevail then, but not before.

Don't love or can't love or won't love

I suspect most of us have been there at some point. Most of us have shared the aversion to mercy that Jesus encountered in his audience. Sometimes people cause us so much pain that we'd rather beat them to a pulp than consider the notion of showing lenience.

I've certainly been there. Maybe we all have. So I under-stand. I have a lot of mercy for people who can't show mercy, especially when it comes to violence or sexual abuse that was covered up or never resolved. Often the truth needs to come out before we can begin the journey of coming to terms with it, let alone consider mercy.

We may fear that we'll make ourselves vulnerable to further pain if we show mercy. Mercy doesn't mean that we have to put ourselves again into the hands of those who hurt us. Neverthe-less, at times we may have to accept that we're unable to take a merciful attitude right now. Maybe the time for mercy has not yet come. Maybe we'll be open to it later.

This is probably why we're tempted to swerve around Jesus' teaching on mercy. It's a big ask. It gets us thinking about all those people we don't love, or can't love, or won't love. It brings to mind those semi-miraculous stories of mercy we hear about on the evening news. The father forgiving the gunman who took his daughter. The political prisoner forgiving his torturers. The orphan forgiving the soldiers who destroyed her village. We're reminded of the virtuosos of mercy, the Gandhis and Mandellas who absorb the violence of their enemies so as to unify their people. It seems too much for us. We may as well not even try.

But I have a suggestion.

Let's take on mercy as an experiment. Instead of looking at the limits of our mercy, why not explore it's possibilities? Instead of thinking of the people we can't bring ourselves to forgive, why not start with those we can? Instead of bemoaning our inability to fathom the farther reaches of mercy, why not stay closer to home?

The virtuosos of mercy surely started somewhere. We shouldn't be put off by the fact that they're more practised and accomplished at it than we are. Let's see if mercy works with the people we rub shoulders with each day. And if it does, maybe we can take it further from there. Let's learn the rigging before we push the boat out.

Generosity bordering on the immoral

To be fair though, the beatitude about mercy is unusual. Jesus says, "Blessed are the merciful for they will receive mercy." It's unusual because he's promising us the same as the characteristic he commends to us. He's implying that there's something about being merciful that somehow opens us to receive mercy from God.

The mercy of God is a consistent theme in the life and teaching of Jesus. He shows us a God inclined to lavish reckless mercy on us, a generosity bordering on the immoral. No matter who we are, no matter what we've done, no matter what we think of ourselves – there is mercy for you and I. There is open space and freedom. God can be moved by us. We could call that Jesus' first lesson in mercy.

But there's something else – a second lesson. Being able to receive this mercy from God, being able to live it and enjoy the freedom of it, requires us to adopt an attitude of mercy too. We're not being offered a deal as such: give mercy and you'll get mercy; you scratch my back and I'll scratch yours. It's more that the life of mercy is a single movement. Living mercy, according to Jesus, isn't possible without also giving mercy.

If Jesus is right then mercy is one of those qualities, like love, that we can receive only to the extent that we give it away ourselves. By showing mercy to other people we somehow have a chance of opening up a world of mercy and freedom for ourselves. Showing and receiving mercy are all of a piece. It's all one country.

The opposite is perhaps also true. When we lack mercy it's as if we've caught our opponent in an imaginary bear-trap. We can visualise the sweet moment of victory when we tell them how it is. We can rehearse getting even or having the last word. We don't need to let them go until we've vented our spleen entirely.

But Jesus wants to free the prisoners of our consciousness. He alerts us to the fact that we're wasting our energy. We're channelling all our initiative and creativity into a vengeful fantasy. And with the words of this beatitude, he opens a door on the torture chamber of our own making and beckons us into a world beyond it. He tells us that the merciful receive mercy. If we free the captives in our mind, we'll be free ourselves.

This is what it means to live mercifully: to free the people we've held hostage. We let them go. We let them be. We recognise that they don't actually need permission from us to be as they are.

A monarch who'd leap off his throne

Mercy is therefore one of the most revolutionary movements of which a human heart is capable. It spells freedom for the people around us – even the people we'd consider above us and there-fore not needful of our mercy. It's freedom for parents and teachers. Freedom for bosses and church leaders. Freedom for brothers and sisters. Freedom for neighbours and colleagues. Freedom for anyone on whom we wish to bestow mercy.

The practice of mercy can also free us to relate to God. The discipline of constantly freeing ourselves from our grievances can change the quality of our relationship to heaven. Instead of perhaps seeing God as the referee in a high school football match who's only worth addressing when things go wrong, he becomes much more than that. When we dissolve the wall of enmity that stands between ourselves and others, we can end up facing a God who's equally disposed to overcoming any-thing that stands between us.

Mercy allows us to play with childlike abandon across the battle lines we'd previously defended or hidden behind. And when we do so it seems God can't help but join in. According to Jesus, that's just the way he is. Not just a referee, but a playmate. A monarch who'd leap off his throne for the chance of seeing us free together.

Mundane mercy

The kind of mercy I'd like to experiment with, therefore, is the normal average everyday kind. Common or garden mercy. The sort that can be found everywhere, that sneaks around under our noses. It's as common as air but without it all our relationships lack breathing space. It's this kind of mercy we can toy with in the God Lab – mundane mercy for the offences, affronts, insults and obstructions of everyday life.

And once we start thinking about mercy like this, we realise it's not that alien to us. It's not an extraterrestrial attitude reserved for saints and martyrs, but a virtue that can pilot us every day. Once we're attuned to it we realise that barely a day goes by without a chance to be secretly merciful to someone or other. The colleague who viciously opposes us in the staff meeting. The mother who boasts at the school gate. The spouse who brings up old mistakes in current arguments. The salesman who takes our money for substandard goods. The motorist who swears at us when we drive. In all these situations, and situations like them, we feel diminished in some way. We've been mistreated, misjudged, undervalued. We've not been seen as a human being. We've not been heard as a credible voice. We're just an enemy, an acolyte, a screw-up, a mark, a liability and little more.

Again we meet the paradox of mercy in everyday life. Mercy often only applies to people who have shown us precious little mercy. Mercy means not treating others as they have treated us. Not returning like for like. Not retaliating tit-for-tat.

Mercy also affects the way we speak about people, particularly when they're not there. Gossip can be so deeply rewarding, especially when it centres around some common enemy and how terrible they are. It's a way of getting even without the risk of actually doing anything. It make us feel a little more important, a little less powerless, a little less afraid for a while. We reduce and simplify our enemies to cardboard cut-outs that can no longer make a claim on our compassion. We populate the world with lifeless scarecrows that can no longer defeat or outmanoeuvre us.

But in the process we no longer feel obliged to learn or stretch our imaginations to the point of understanding people we don't like. We miss the opportunity to become more effective and creative in our dealings with the world. Mercy offers us a chance of getting a better understanding of the people around us, but only by giving up the tendency to wish they didn't exist or needing them to be different.

Take the fifth

According to Jesus then, when we show mercy we not only free others, but free ourselves too. We no longer see a world of blockades and cordons, of principles and barriers, but of human possibilities. We see people of flesh and bone and living tissue, rather than immovable statues. Our willingness to listen and learn and grow invites others to do the same if they wish to. And consequently we see the ruthless aspects of the world infected with freedom and flexibility. This is a hypothesis we can now test for ourselves.

Do we become more effective in relating to people when we give up the need to make them wrong? Can we exchange our annoyance for deftness and skill, and a greater reach and colour to our imagination in understanding people? That's the test. Do we live freedom when we give freedom?

So let's take the fifth. The fifth experiment, that is.

Experiment 5:

Think of someone who needs your mercy. Don't choose your worst enemy, but someone you can imagine extending a bit of mercy to: someone you feel aggrieved at perhaps or mildly offended by. Someone you struggle to relate to. Someone you talk or think about in less than complimentary terms. It could be anyone: a friend, a colleague, a family member. Identify an easy target for mercy.

Get curious. If you can, put aside for a moment the offensive comment, or the intimidating anger, or your general annoyance with them. Rather than thinking about how you'd like to get back at them, think about how you might reason or negotiate with them as a friend. How might you make your point or express your opinion to them? Create a movie in your mind about interacting with the person and being respected by them. Enjoy it and replay it as many times as you like. It's kind of a visual prayer. It's the future you'd like to happen.

Change the conversation. If you've tended to talk critically about them behind their back, start to alter this conversation too. Don't gloss over the difficulties in the relationship, but start to talk about them creatively. Instead of complaining about how wrong the person is, start to talk about how you might befriend them or get them on side. Freely acknowledge the difficulty or fear involved in trying this.

Pray for them. Whenever you find yourself thinking about them, offer a short, positive prayer for both you and they. Examples could be: "Father, grant us love" or "God, bring us security" or "Lord, give us hope." Come up with a short phrase that sums up the way you'd like the relationship to be. Speak this out to God any time you feel bothered by the situation.

Watch. As you think and pray and talk this way, notice any opportunities that emerge to improve your relationship with them. It may not happen all at once, but keep an eye open for any movement in the relationship. Notice also any changes this brings about in you, paying particular attention to any sense of increased freedom you experience as a result. Even if you never see them again, you can still practice mercy and release yourself from holding a grudge.

Repeat. Practicing mercy in this way is rarely a one-off event. We often need to repeat our thoughts, words and prayers to see them take effect. Feel free to cycle through these points as often as seems necessary.

The gentle massage

Mercy can bring space and freedom to situations that have been locked down. If a grudge is like emotional muscle cramp, then mercy is the gentle massage that allows us to release our grasp.

A few years ago I returned to work after a fortnight on holiday to discover a pile of dirty coffee cups on a tray in the middle of the floor in our office. The nurses and psychologists who shared the room were all busily tapping away at their computers or silently studying case files, seemingly oblivious to the fact that a tower of crockery was now the centre piece of our open plan office.

It had clearly been there a while. Some of the cups were going mouldy and the pile seemed to have become a sort of proxy notice board for the team. There were four or five scraps of paper attached to it saying things like, "this is disgusting", "someone should clear these up", "how vile!" etc.

Before I knew it I was in the kitchen washing them up. It was only when I returned the coffee cups to their usual place that I realised I'd committed a subversive act in the eyes of the team. Someone – no one had yet admitted to it – had used up all the cups for a meeting a few days before and failed to wash them up afterwards. A standoff had ensued in which no one would wash them until the perpetrator handed themselves in. No one could drink coffee until the guilty party incriminated themselves. On reflex, out of complete ignorance of this history, I'd crossed the line and done what needed to be done.

Washing those cups was an act of ignorance. But sometimes mercy looks a bit like ignorance. It fails to see the history or pain that has gone before. It remembers them, but doesn't allow them to cloud the present. It crosses the line. It leaps the hedge that separates us from other people and cocks a snoot at the distinctions we draw between ourselves and others. Mercy frees us to live rightly, rather than die for being right.

focus

Words ringing in my ears

The beatitude that Jesus speaks about next is the one that currently challenges me most. It bothers me. It keeps me up at night. It shakes the foundations of my current way of living. The words ringing in my ears right now are those Jesus spoke in the sixth beatitude. They sound like this:

> Blessed are the pure in heart
> for they will see God.

The heart, according to Jesus, isn't just the large muscle that pumps blood around our bodies. Nor is it the fluffy pink love heart we see on valentines cards. The heart as Jesus talks about it is the centre of our motivations. It's the seat of out intentions. It's the place where we deliberate and make decisions.

The images of the blood pumping muscle and the pink love heart aren't entirely wrong. The heart *is* the source of our life force. It's the origin of our love for others. But it's much more than that. The heart is the centre of our life. It encompasses the things we hold dear, the commitments we live and die for. Our heart is our core.

The Danish philosopher Søren Kierkegaard once wrote a short book based on this beatitude. He called it, *Purity of Heart is to Will One Thing*. For him, purity of heart meant clarity and focus and passion in living. So when Jesus blesses the pure in heart, he's blessing a clear-sighted and uncontaminated approach to life.

It's a massive challenge to me (and could be to you too). I'll tell you why.

The hundred tiny compromises

But first a problem.

For some reason, the phrase pure in heart has a fairytale feel for me. It seems to belong to stories where knights in shining armour battle dark forces, dragons and occasionally man-eating vegetation to reach a princess locked in a tower. Purity of heart for some reason brings these images to mind.

And both characters seem pure to me. The knight is pure because he won't allow anything to stop him from saving the princess he loves. The princess is pure because she's removed from the world, helplessly locked away in a tower waiting to be saved.

It offers two ways of being pure in heart. We can be pure like the knight by knowing the trials and temptations of the world, but fighting them. We can be pure by resisting the temptation to compromise for the sake of comfort or safety. Or we can be pure like the princess, by not knowing the world and thereby not being contaminated by it.

If I had to choose, I think I'd prefer the active purity of the knight rather than the passive purity of the princess. And in the world around me I see both kinds of purity in both men and women. I know men who've sought purity by retreating from the world and women who show purity by battling dragons of corporate greed and governmental corruption.

But the problem is this: it doesn't matter which flavour of purity I go with, the active or the passive kind, I'm confronted with my failure to qualify for the title. I'm all too keenly aware of how easily intimidated I am. Of how quickly I give up in the face of hardship and opposition. How often I comply when I should resist. How often I remain silent when I should be speaking out. What bothers me are the hundred tiny compromises that settle in my heart like dust in a cold hearth.

If my heart were ever tried by a fair and impartial judge it'd be unlikely to read: 100% pure. That's why this beatitude challenges me so sharply. I feel it's aimed at me.

A soft spot for rebels

Perhaps I feel targeted by Jesus because the beatitudes were aimed at people: real people with real lives and real concerns. They weren't just timeless principles, they were laser-guided messages fired with pinpoint accuracy into the hearts of the crowd. Jesus was reading the faces of the thousands in front of him and responding to their needs. He was speaking to you and I.

And if that is the case, it's interesting to wonder who he aimed this line at. Who did Jesus wink at knowingly when he blessed the pure hearted?

It could have been that he saw a political rebel, a zealot with a sword at his belt. We know that Jesus didn't endorse violence or political uprising. He couldn't sign up to the cause the rebel represented. He wasn't able to justify the means. But perhaps he could still bless the purity with which some people pursue their ends. Perhaps, like me, he had a soft spot for rebels. Perhaps he couldn't help smiling at the raw passion for truth and justice that the political revolutionary embodied – a passion that some people might call single-mindedness or even purity of heart.

If this were the case, then this beatitude is a blessing on those who are willing to follow a cause to the end; those who are prepared to organise their lives around a single vision. It's an acknowledgement of those willing to stick their necks out for the sake of a better world. It's a blessing on all those who are prepared to shed dead-weight so as to run unencumbered by anything irrelevant to the commitment they've made. It doesn't commend the fanaticism of the zealot, but it does invite us to de-clutter our lives with a view to becoming a disciple.

Before we got clever

On the other hand, it's equally possible that when Jesus blessed the pure in heart he was looking not into the narrow eyes of a dissident, but into the wide eyes of a child. Perhaps he spoke these words to everyone while tussling the hair of the nearest toddler or grinning at a baby in its mother's arms.

My youngest son, Tom, is ten months old. And I seem to spend almost all my time with him bouncing on my knee, playing hide and seek, or rolling about on the carpet. We spend a lot of time just staring at each other, checking each other out. Right now he's particularly fascinated by my nose, which given its size I can understand.

When we gaze at each other I don't know what he sees in my eyes. Love, I hope. But when I look into his eyes I often get the impression of looking into clear pools of water. Nothing is hidden. He hasn't yet learned the art of concealing himself. Sometimes I see delight and laughter and joy. Sometimes pain or displeasure. But almost always wonder. Everything in the world is full of fascination for him. A door, a blanket, a watch, a spoon, a pen, can keep him occupied for hours, just holding, just staring, just wondering.

And this too is purity. Not the ideological purity of the

fanatic who will kill for their cause. But the purity of the child, for whom everything is seen for the first time.

And it makes me wonder. Perhaps in blessing the pure in heart Jesus is inviting us to return to that childlike kind of purity – to a state of wonder. He's commending those who retain the ability to be surprised. He's inviting us to look at the world again with fresh eyes; to shed for a moment the weary perspective we've grown accustomed to. Perhaps we're being reminded how the world looked before we grew tired of it. Before we got clever and calculating and cynical.

Jesus is blessing the uncontaminated heart. Both the child and the rebel believe in a beautiful world. The rebel dreams of a beautiful world where oppression is lifted. The child lives in a world that is beautiful already.

The glimmer of God

A fanatical focus, the focus of the rebel, can let us down. Our agenda, the purpose we serve in life, dictates the way we perceive things. It illuminates some things, but it can blind us to others. A focus is a way of seeing, but it can also be a way of not seeing.

It's said that when Captain Cook first sailed into Botany Bay, the indigenous people went about their business as usual, seemingly oblivious to the ship weighing anchor just off the shore. Because they'd never seen anything like it before they were simply unable to see it. It didn't exist as far as they were concerned. They took notice when the smaller boats were lowered from the deck and rowed towards land. If something lies entirely outside our experience we may not be able to see it at all.

Jesus faced the same problem with many of his contemporaries. They were utterly devoted to the idea that they were God's own people, his favourites if you like. And they therefore assumed that if God was up to anything at all, he was hatching a plan to get imperial Rome off their back. For many of them freedom from Rome and the rising of the Israelite nation to become a God-established super-power were what God was up to. As a consequence, anything that corresponded to this agenda was viewed as going with God. Anything that frustrated or compromised this goal was viewed as going against God.

This was the lens through which Jesus was assessed by his own people in his own time. It was the criteria by which they measured him. It was the gauge by which they decided whether he spoke for God or not. And it's also why, when he refused to be crowned head of a violent rebellion, he was viewed as a disappointment, a failure and an irrelevance to many of his countrymen.

Only those who could separate themselves from nationalistic interest, who could step back from the need for violence, were able to see the glimmer of God in Jesus of Nazareth. Only those willing to be surprised, provoked, challenged and changed would see God in what he was about. Only those with a childlike purity of heart would see the beauty in him.

A gift in the lap of the pure in heart

Jesus wasn't scared to talk about himself. He wasn't worried about making himself the subject of his stories or taking prophecies from hundreds of years previously and claiming that they were about him. He didn't seem to worry that this could be offensive or come across as egotistical. He said it as he saw it.

And therefore everything he says and does tell us something about who he is. The beatitudes are, in a sense, all about him: who he is, what he represents and what he's come to do.

But this one is especially about him.

When Jesus says the pure in heart will see God, he perhaps meant primarily that they'd see God in him; they'd see God in what he was up to. But only those who could free themselves from the assumption that God and patriotism were the same thing stood a chance. Only those who could take a pure, unsullied look at Jesus would see God in him.

And this, according to the stories, is what slowly dawned on his disciples. They came to believe that Jesus not only represented God like a messenger, or resembled him like a holy man, but that he somehow *was* God. They came to believe that in some strange way the source of the universe became human in Jesus. The Ancient One was born like a human being, grew up like a human being, walked and talked, and made a living, and shared his life with other people like a human being. They came to believe that Jesus was God embodied, incarnated in flesh and blood.

It was a big leap for them – a paradigm shift in their thinking. It was an occurrence that changed their perception of everything; an insight that could only land as a gift in the lap of the pure in heart.

He's also a star

It was a big leap for his disciples to see Jesus as God. It's a big leap for us too. And one we may not be able to take too quickly. We'll need to be at least marginally acquainted with Jesus before we can trust him. And if we do come to the conclusion that he's God, and therefore worthy of our allegiance, it's likely to land on us in a sudden moment of insight. It's like a breath of inspiration or an epiphany. Some people would call it a revelation.

Perhaps you've had the experience of searching the house for something you've lost, like a wallet or car keys. We walk from room to room scanning all the open surfaces for the thing we're missing. And then on our fourth or fifth trip into the dining room we see it lying in plain sight on the table in front of us. It had always been there and yet for some reason it had been invisible to us. We feel bewildered and surprised. How could we have not seen this before? It was so obviously in front of our eyes the whole time and yet we were unable to see it.

This is like the experience Jesus' disciples had in beginning to realise who he was. It can also be the way knowing Jesus occurs to us too. It's like suddenly discovering that the guy we've been hanging out with is actually an international celebrity. We knew him first as a friend, someone we liked and admired. We only later learn that he's also a star.

But for the time being we're just getting to know him. We're just getting acquainted. If there's something more, a revelation to be had, we can wait for it. Right now in the God Lab, we just set the conditions in which lightning might strike.

The art of everyday God-spotting

The sixth beatitude, therefore, is the one where the rubber hits the road. Ultimately, the concern of most of us wild-haired, white-coated residents of the God Lab is to know God. And that's what this beatitude promises to the pure in heart.

But what does it mean to see God? And how would purity of heart help us?

Jesus is talking about himself in the sixth beatitude. He blesses the pure in heart for seeing God in him. But he's also, I think, talking about the condition of heart needed to see God anywhere in anyone; the attitude required to push past the humble and sometimes offensive forms in which God appears in everyday life. The pure in heart see God everywhere.

Most people who claim to see God aren't talking about an open-eyed vision of a heavenly person. Admittedly, there are some people who claim to have seen God or angels or heaven like that – in the same way they'd see you or I as light through their retina. I can't make any claims like that for myself and, having worked on psychiatric wards for over a decade, I'm cautious about giving too much credence to mystical visions. But I don't have to believe all such claims to be open to the possibility that people occasionally meet God face to face.

Yet, when Jesus spoke of seeing God, I don't think he was talking about a mystical apparition like that. It's much more likely that he was referring not only to himself, but to seeing God at work in the everyday affairs of life. He doesn't discount supernatural appearances, but treats them as part of the weave of everyday life when they do occur.

On one occasion Jesus explained the basic principle by which he operated. He said he just did whatever he saw his father doing – his Heavenly Father that is. That's the way Jesus ticked. He kept a look out for God's action in the world and joined in.

Seeing God in the world is not as difficult as we might think. We just have to want to see him. People I know who are well practiced in the art of everyday God-spotting seem to spend most of their time just asking one thing: "God, what are you doing right now?" And as a result all kinds of coincidences and intuitions seem to come their way. They dream that they must phone a friend or write a letter or visit the local pub landlord. Or they find themselves inexplicably compelled to step outside the house, only to bump into a long lost friend. They know things they shouldn't about friends who are sick and strangers who are distressed or secrets that privately torture the person sat next to them on the bus. Constantly asking God to show himself as they do, they can't help seeing him in action and joining in. God starts to share his concerns with them. It's almost as if they become God's co-workers in caring for the world.

But it's their purity of heart that makes this possible: their perpetual focus on God; their desire to see him in the minutiae of each day – in every person who crosses their path, every problem or frustration they encounter, every brush with the natural world. God, it appears, can be met in all of these, as long as we have the eyes to see him.

Currency for impressing people

Nowhere is this kind of purity more needed than in the world of religion and spirituality.

What starts off as a desire to know God can quickly get side-tracked. We perhaps open ourselves to God because we feel we need to. It seems a good thing to do, a necessity even. It satisfies. It comforts. It challenges. It's worthwhile. We may start out with God purely and simply for the sake of making contact with the divine. We want to find a spiritual resting place, somewhere to belong in the universe.

But then in a church community, or with our closest friends, we start to earn credentials for being spiritual. We get called the spiritual one or the prayerful one. We may even get invited to talk or lecture or run workshops.

Then, if we're not careful, the order of our spiritual life gets reversed. Instead of loving God and therefore gaining insights to share with other people, we start going to God just so we can have something to share. The purity of our first love gets contaminated by the prospect of being applauded. We may even spend our most private moments with God daydreaming about how our stories of intimacy and exploits with him will go down when we tell them to the crowd. Our public persona infringes on our most intimate moments with God. We lose the purity of our hearts.

Whenever I've prayed or read the Bible recently, I've found myself resorting to the words, "God, I want to know you." It's

a heartfelt prayer, often prayed a bit desperately, in full awareness of the large part of myself that would like to use my experience and knowledge of God as currency for impressing
people – or at least impressing the sort of people who are
impressed by that kind of thing.

Praying that prayer (I want to know you) is a way of remind-
ing myself and God that when push comes to shove that's what
I want. On a good day, when I'm neither panicked nor insecure
nor guilty, I want to know God. And if a million distractions
and fantasies of popularity bar the way, then I at least want to
want to know God.

It's an acknowledgment that in the end I know that meeting
God in the purest, simplest terms, without publicity or fanfare,
is the only spiritual experience that will do me any good. It's
the only spiritual experience that will go some way to making
me good. It's a desire for purity of heart.

Out-and-about prayer

So this is our experiment. To take on purity of heart and see if
in doing so, we do indeed see God.

Experiment 6:

Pick one of the prayers alluded to in this chapter.
You could try, "God, I want to see you." Or, "God, I
want to know you." Or, "God, show me what you're
up to." Or a variation on this theme. The idea is
that you find a phrase that suits you in asking to
see God in daily life. If you're not sure, just find a
quiet moment and pray a couple of them. Choose
the one that gets closest to feeling right to you.

This is an out-and-about prayer. The experiment
involves sowing it consistently and quietly through

your daily routine. So you may want to find some kind of reminder or memory-aid that will jog your memory to pray it regularly throughout the day. You could put an asterisk by each item in your diary or a card by the kettle or set some reminders on your mobile phone. Whenever you see the prompt, take a second to connect with God and pray the prayer.

If you have time, pause after praying and notice anything that occurs immediately afterwards. You may find that you want to go somewhere or see someone or read something. Just notice any thoughts, images or impulses that arise in you. You can decide what to do with them. And if nothing like that comes, don't worry too much.

Practice praying like this over a week or so, paying special attention to anything that strikes you as unusual or exceptional over the course of the week: coincidences that happen, conversations that go deeper than usual, people who come into your life, opportunities to care or to grow that come your way. You can decide for yourself if you see God in any of these things.

If you do see God over the course of the week and it seems appropriate, you may like to thank him for revealing himself to you. Use the fact that you think you've seen something of him as an impetus for praying to see more. You may be entering into the divine game of hide-and-seek by which God woos you into knowing him more. When we chase God with all our heart, we tend to find him.

God's already out there

There was a time in my life when I aimed to carry God through my day. It was an admirable aspiration, I think. I just wanted to remain conscious of him in every moment of the day. But it never quite worked. Within two seconds of arriving at work, I was completely immersed in the demands of the day and barely gave God a thought until lunch, when I realised I'd been spiritually oblivious for hours.

But it started to dawn on me that God's existence didn't depend on my concentration. He didn't disappear in a puff of smoke the moment I thought about something else. Irrespective of my attentiveness to him, God often came running to meet me over the course of the day – an answered prayer, a remarkable conversation, a gesture of kindness, a moment of courage or peace. I began to trust that God was in my day whether I knew it or not.

My premise had been wrong. I didn't need to carry God through my day. He wasn't some poor cripple who needed my help to get about. God's already out there, dancing and weaving and doing his thing. And if I have the eyes to notice him, I can join in.

Maybe you could too.

engage

The kind of peace I could do with

One of the disadvantages of choosing to live in a city is that you don't get to choose your neighbours. People living quite different lifestyles rub shoulders in close proximity, separated only by a few lines of brick and plaster dust. In a city, you don't get to choose your neighbours, but you often can't help hearing what's going on next door – especially if it's at high volume.

We've lived in three houses since we married. And over the years we've shared our walls with a diverse range of people. Our back catalogue of next door neighbours includes a working prostitute with bipolar disorder, a small army of Lithuanian factory workers, a student fan of drum and bass, an alcoholic couple who re-enacted fight club on weekends, a gay strip club employee, a German lawyer and a local politician-cum-guitar teacher. All of them have been our neighbours and, to a certain extent, our friends.

But, as a consequence, peace – the theme of our next experiment – has often been a prominent concern for me. We chose to live in the city because we wanted to be where the action was. We wanted to live close to people of all kinds. We wanted to position ourselves to know and care about the people in our community. And we do.

But sometimes I could just do with some peace and quiet – a secluded haven away from it all. A sanctuary uninterrupted by the sounds of screaming or sex or cymbals. The noise that reverberates through our walls can be an unwelcome invasion of an otherwise tranquil living space. It can be an inconvenience, an interruption I could do without. It's easy to wish that it would just go away. Or even that my neighbours would just go away.

That's the kind of peace I could do with. The peace that comes from the absence of noise, the absence of disturbance, the absence of conflict. The peace that comes from having no one demand anything from me. The peace I yearn for is nothing really (no sound, no music, no laughter, no fighting, no contact), just silence.

Everything made well

But that's not the kind of peace Jesus had in mind when he spoke the seventh beatitude:

> Blessed are the peacemakers,
> for they will be called sons of God.

When Jesus talked about peace or peacemaking he was yet again drawing from a deep well in the spiritual consciousness of his people. The Hebrew word for peace was *shalom*. It was a greeting, meaning both welcome and farewell, but it was also the word the Hebrew prophets had settled on to describe the golden age to come. Shalom meant *everything made well*. Not just the absence of disruption, but the advent of harmony.

In blessing the peacemaker Jesus was no doubt alluding to the all-encompassing notion of *shalom*. He's blessing those who are willing to be agents or constructors of that kind of peace. His blessing seems to be aimed at those who take an active role in propagating peace, who take it upon themselves to parachute into conflict and weave peace out of the tangled threads that surround them. He's blessing peace*makers* rather than peace-*keepers* – people willing to risk something just to make peace, rather than those fearing to risk anything just to keep it.

For a while I was involved in treating military personnel suffering psychological trauma following active service. One of the consistent reports I received from the soldiers I worked with was that peacekeeping missions, where the army acted as a buffer between opposing forces, were more stressful on the troops than out and out warfare. At least in street to street fighting lives were risked for the sake of an objective to be won. But in peacekeeping operations, the tension of constant danger ground on for days without reprieve, with troops never really knowing when the next ambush might come.

Contrary to what we might think, it's harder to be a peace-*keeper* than a peace*maker*. Even in everyday civilian relationships peace*keeping* can be an arduous and demanding activity. We tiptoe around other people as if they're landmines of disapproval about to go off; anticipating displeasure before it occurs so as to plan evasive manoeuvres; choosing compliance and silence so as not to create social awkwardness; offering false flatteries to keep things on an even keel. This is the energy-intensive face of peace*keeping* in everyday life. It's not what Jesus is advising when he blesses the peacemakers.

Peacemaking is so different from peacekeeping. Keeping peace means preserving the status quo. Making peace means creating something different, bringing something new into being. It's an active endeavour that brings all the skill we can gather to the task of giving something good to the people around us.

It applies to everyone we have contact with – even people we know only as decibels through the wall, or a voice on the phone, or a uniform at the supermarket checkout. In its most basic form peacemaking looks a lot like courtesy: a willingness to understand and treat people as human beings. It's a reversal of the tendency to treat other people as objects, particularly those people who inconvenience us or get in our way.

Some of the attitudes we've looked at already, like mercy and purity of heart, are the early symptoms of peacemaking. But it develops from there. In its later stages, it's the risk we take to repair relationships that have gone sour, the emotional courage involved in trying to bail out friendships or marriages that have taken in water.

Further down the line, in its advanced stages, peacemaking is rabidly contagious. It goes looking for trouble. It seeks conflict to resolve. It directs itself towards people we've only ever known as strangers or competitors or objects of scorn. It builds bridges and forges alliances between people who'd never normally meet or speak.

Peacemaking, in its wild virulent state, takes the bull by the horns. Instead of observing fearfully, it gets involved. Instead of fleeing conflict, it moves towards it. It sees the people implicated and engages them. Peacemaking attempts to befriend those we previously held at arm's length with the aim of making things better for everyone.

The walls that separate us are all too thin

Most of us don't choose to become peacemakers as such. We don't set out to change the world. Most of the time we just find ourselves confronted with a distressing or unacceptable situation that leaves us at a loss. We don't know what to do. We gather information and talk to friends. We may even throw our hands up to God and say, "What would you have me do here?" This is often the beginning of our peacemaking. The moment we address heaven with a direct question like that we've effectively volunteered to become peacemakers.

Peacemaking more than anything involves a change of perspective. For me it means starting to think about my home situation in a different way. With regard to my neighbours, it means starting to explore what it would be like to make peace rather than just need it. What would it be like to view the intrusion of noise and disruption from my neighbours not just as a problem to be solved, but as an open door to be entered? Not just an inconvenience to be rid of, but an invitation to get involved?

So when I head to the outhouse with some laundry, only to find underwear in the washing machine that doesn't belong to us, it's no longer just an opportunity to confront the person who's been using our appliance on the sly. It's a gift. A moment of contact. A chance to start a conversation with the young woman next door about how we can help her, and how she can use our washing machine if she really needs to.

And when the students next door crank up the volume in the early hours of the morning and I go down in my dressing gown to shut them up, I again take it as an invitation. The awkward exchange on the doorstep is just the beginning of an ongoing conversation. Perhaps even the start of a friendship in which I pop round with a card and champagne to celebrate the start of term and they come to understand that loud music in the middle of the night may not be a huge blessing to a young family.

And then when the woman in the downstairs flat comes knocking for money for the electricity meter and I know she really wants it for alcohol, it's a chance to enquire about how things are with her and offer some help that isn't directly financial.

We give her details of our friendly neighbourhood debt advisor and somewhere she can get food if she needs it.

These are just some of the minor ways we've attempted to proliferate peace over the last few months. They're our efforts to love our neighbours as we love ourselves.

Peacemaking it seems, looks for the receptivity in other people. Like water seeking the lowest point, it relentlessly probes for the possibility of friendship. It assumes that no one is beyond the pale. No one is entirely lost or so broken that they can't respond with kindness to a humble human request. It assumes that peace is not imposed by force, but created between people as they agree on how to live together.

An act of peace appeals to the better aspects of our nature, it gives us an opportunity to get closer to being the people we'd like to be. It recognises that the walls that separate us are all too thin and that somehow we belong together.

Peacemaking is presumptuous

But it doesn't always work. Sometimes our desire for peace with other people backfires. The door on which we knock is slammed in our face. And so there's a reticence in me when it comes to the idea of being a peacemaker. When I need to step forward and create peace, when I need to stand up and be counted, some apprehension stands up with me.

It doesn't matter how big or small the act of peacemaking may be. Whether I'm dealing with noisy neighbours or silencing students or campaigning against building plans or volunteering at a soup kitchen or debriefing asylum seekers or sitting with street children. No matter how large or small the peacemaking is, it doesn't come easily to me. It feels unfamiliar and dis-concerting – a bit of a stretch. And afterwards I feel like I've pretended to be bigger and stronger than I actually am. Like a kid strutting around in his dad's shoes.

But at the same time, I'm conflicted. There's another force at work in me. I may feel intimidated and inadequate at the prospect of working for peace, but I still *want* to be there. I don't know if I'll live through it, but I know I can't quite live without it. I feel propelled towards being a peacemaker.

Somehow, if I'm going to follow Jesus, it seems this is the dangerous trail he's pointing me towards. If I'm going to follow him I need to do so even in the places that are strange or foreign or frightening to me. Not just the well-worn sunlit paths, but into the thickets and briars, the places I habitually avoid and wouldn't venture into were he not somewhere ahead beckoning me. It's all very well sticking with Jesus when he walks on dry ground, but what about when he walks on water?

The thing about peacemaking that frightens me is that it involves interfering with other people's lives – getting involved in danger and conflict that I've sought out. It hasn't come to my door, I've gone looking for it. So if I get hurt or rejected or even killed I have no one to blame but myself.

Peacemaking is presumptuous. It means that I (often with friends) have decided to get involved in something that isn't really my fight. Whether a neighbourhood dispute or an international conflict, I've elected to step into the middle of someone else's war. And in doing so I leave myself open to the accusation of being a busybody, an interferer or an egotist.

The attempt to befriend some people will no doubt make enemies of others and I'm therefore painting myself as a target in a hostile situation. So when it comes to peacemaking, the thing I fear is not so much the danger involved, but the fact that I've taken it upon myself to do something about it. What troubles me is not the risk, but the question: who do you think you are? I ask it of myself: who do I think I am to get mixed up in matters that don't concern me?

Unwilling to don my cape and tights

If I knew my actions would be effective, it wouldn't bother me quite so much. If I knew my words would bring resolution to the fighting couple next door. If I knew that chaining myself to the tree or lying in front of the bulldozer would stop the demolition. If I knew that my voice would be heard, that my signature would count, that showing my face would matter. If I knew I could make a difference (as I've been told I can) then peacemaking would be a much more attractive idea. If I knew I could change things, I'd feel compelled to act. I'd go giddy on peacemaking and wouldn't be able to stop myself.

But I fear that what I do will make no difference in the world at all – that things will grind on just as they always have, irrespective of my attempts to resist or oppose them. The couple next door will continue to knock seven bells out of each other irrespective of whether I intervene. Bulldozers will roll and trees fall whether I'm attached to them or not.

Psychologists might say I have low self-efficacy. I find it difficult to believe that my actions will make much difference to the world around me. And that's why I'm unwilling to don my cape and tights in an attempt to play the hero. I don't want to try to make a difference because I fear my attempt to stand up and be someone will only confirm that I am in fact no one. In trying to matter I'll discover I don't.

A movement that would outlive the empire

When Jesus talks about his mission on earth it seems that he was aware of this dilemma. His biographies record the many faces of temptation that leered at him in his adult life. Chief among them was the temptation to be more impressive, to win people to himself through showmanship and drama, just to drive home his message. But he didn't choose that route.

He was very fond of talking about himself obliquely. He'd

tell a story or plant an image in the minds of his disciples that at the time must have mystified them. On one occasion he described himself as a seed. He said that a seed could only bear fruit if it fell into the ground and died. He was talking about his own death and his belief that it would be just a beginning – the first green shoots of something entirely new in the world; a silent germination that would grow far beyond the obscure soil of its origin.

Jesus was right about his death. It was inauspicious to say the least. It was designed to put him through hell. To let him know in no uncertain terms that everything he hoped for was over. To convince anyone who might aspire to imitate him that everything he stood for had come to nothing. It was intentionally degrading. He was whipped and tortured, dressed up like a king and mock-worshipped. Just so he would know how far short he fell of that power. Just so he would know that he was nothing, nobody, an insignificant smudge on the pages of history. Just another blot, another anomaly, another fad. An unusable stone in the house of human progress.

We're so used to thinking of Jesus as a great figure in world history that it's difficult to imagine that he didn't look like that at the time. But this act, this death, was Jesus' great moment of peacemaking. It was indeed a seed that would bear fruit across the world and through the ages, a movement that would out-live the empire that destroyed him and be an inspiration to anyone like you or me who fears that their efforts to make a better world could be in vain. It was a lesson for those who fear that nothing will be changed by making their bed in front of the relentless bulldozer of progress.

Prepared to leap into living hell

Jesus blessed the peacemakers by calling them *sons of God.* That's what happened to him. One of the guards who mocked and spat at him during the execution watched him breathe his last and had a change of heart. Something about the way Jesus died got to him and he blurted out for all to hear that Jesus truly was the Son of God.

There was something about the death of Jesus that drew amazement from the people who saw it. Perhaps it was his composure under torture or his presence of mind in forgiving his killers as they hammered nails into his wrists. Something about it was exceptional. It was enigmatic. It led people to conclude that this remarkable resolve, this unbreakable soul was somehow unworldly. It came from beyond himself. It had divine origins.

It was an act of peace because it presented the people of his time with another way. An alternative to the eternally conflicting forces of oppression and revolution. Jesus refused to be caught up in the political squabbles of his day and thereby sought to bridge the gap between people. There was a way of peace that could change the world.

But more than that, he also looked to bring an even greater peace. He looked to heal the chasm that had run like a deep fissure between the human world and God. He sought to close the gaping maw that yawned between us and heaven. And if, as his disciples came to believe, Jesus was in fact God living a human life, he showed us the incredible extremes to which God is prepared to go to repair his relationship with us. A God prepared to leap into living hell, to share our torments, just to know us. A God who wants to bring peace to the world and is prepared to pay the price for it.

God's look-alikes

Jesus' action was presumptuous. His willingness to die and draw people to himself wasn't requested or even really understood by many people at the time. It was only as events unfolded that they began to understand exactly what had happened.

He died for us whether we wanted him to or not. He solved a problem we never acknowledged we had. It seems to me that this kind of sacrifice requires an incredible level of confidence. To be willing to throw ourselves on the trash heap of history in the belief that somehow this will make a difference to the world requires an enormous degree of inner certainty. It requires us to believe in the worth of what we do when it would be more expedient to give up and shut up.

And that's the blessing that Jesus offers to those who, like him, take it upon themselves to be peacemakers. Something changes in them. They become fully identified with God's care plan for the world. They become God's look-alikes.

When we step out to make a difference we know it's presumptuous. We know people will point at us and say: who do they think they are to do that? But we also know that in stepping forward to make peace we're stepping into the kind of life we were made for. We're leaving the bench and joining the game. We're grasping God by the hand and accepting his offer to bring something good to some small corner of the universe. We may not look like anything, but we face life with all the prowess of which we are capable. We rise to our full stature.

And maybe occasionally people notice and wonder about the source of our confidence. And maybe even more occasionally someone with a poetic turn of phrase will take it upon themselves to name us. And maybe they'll call us sons of God.

Peacemaking begins at home, but it doesn't end there

Compared to the famine-stricken war zones of the world, the examples I've given here seem trivial. I haven't told stories of nations turned around, or human atrocities ceased, or urban squalor rejuvenated – just a couple of things I did with my wife and a few friends in the neighbourhood. But where else are we to begin? Charity begins at home, they say. Perhaps so too does peacemaking.

As I awaken to the needs on my doorstep, I become more rather than less disturbed by the problems elsewhere. Far from becoming parochial in my concern, I find myself drawn to other places too. Friends already working in Africa and Southeast Asia attract my attention. I start to wonder how I might join them and what I could do to help them. Peacemaking begins at home, but it doesn't end there.

This experiment is therefore presented in a spirit of starting where you are. What could you do to take up the cause of peace on your doorstep? That's the theme of our next spiritual exercise.

Experiment 7:

Think about a recurrent situation that causes you frustration or annoyance. It could be noisy neighbours or a disagreeable colleague or a relationship in need of repair. Pick an example of something like this that you'd like to change and can imagine being different. It's important that you want it to change and believe that it could. It may be something that you've put up with until recently, but would now like to see move on.

Write down the person or problem on a piece of card and put it by your bed. Every time you go to bed or wake up look at the card and pray peace over what's written there. Do it briefly. You may want to say something like, "Father, bring peace to this situation" or "God, I pray for peace for x." Find a form of words that works for you. You can write them down verbatim on the card if you wish to. You may even like to imagine beaming or willing peace towards the situation you've written down.

Do some watchful waiting. Keep a look out for opportunities to change the situation. It could be that it changes spontaneously while you're praying, seemingly of its own accord. It could also be that opportunities arise to intervene in the situation, that conversations or meetings spring up out of nowhere. If these seem like a chance to say something or move things on in some way, do so if you feel able to.

If you find you've been praying peace over something and nothing seems to be happening, you may want to change the scenario you're praying into for something that seems a bit easier. The key to this kind of praying is to start small.

Keep an eye out for peace. If you see peace come to some small situation, you may like to offer a thank you to God for this. View it as an encouragement to try your hand at praying for larger issues where the stakes are higher. When you've finished praying over one card swap it for another in which you'd like some peace to come. Keep doing this for as long as seems worthwhile.

Tiny bonds of peace

Perhaps I could end with another gentle story about making peace. It comes from my single days when I was sharing a house with someone who I liked a great deal, but was slowly drifting apart from. This friend of mine had lost his job and was becoming increasingly depressed and morose. Each evening I'd return home to find him slumped in front of the TV: volume at full-blast, remote control in hand, staring lifelessly at the screen, barely watching.

I was starting to get depressed too. All my efforts to move things on, to make him laugh or talk or go out, were met with grunting or silence. He just sat there mesmerised by the television. I started to think that if I could only tear him away from the TV for a moment, I'd be able to engage him and help in some way. But I was pretty sure if I marched in, switched it off and demanded his attention we'd only end up fighting. Somehow I needed him to turn it off by his own choice and do something else.

That's how I found myself praying. One night before falling asleep I haggled in prayer with God. I knew my friend loved listening to music but hadn't done so for months and I found myself asking God if one night he could just prompt my friend to switch off the TV and listen to his stereo. If only he would turn off the box and put on the music at least we'd have a chance to speak.

I can still remember where I was when it happened. I was stood at the kitchen sink, finishing off the evening dishes, when in the next room I heard the familiar blare of the evening schedule fall silent to be replaced, seconds later by the overture of a Broadway musical. I finished the dishes in tears, and when I was done, I made two cups of tea and took them through to the living room. And we talked. I can't say it was a monumental turning point in my friend's fight against depression, but I'd like to think it was at least a moment of peace in the midst of his torment.

How many times a day do things like that happen worldwide? I don't know. They're too inconspicuous to count. So delicate, so unobtrusive, so easy to miss. Maybe the world is held together by thousands of tiny bonds of peace just like this one – those moments when God goes about his business incognito and only a few people know what he's up to. But when we pray for peace we get to be in on the act. We get to know what it's like to be a child in the family business.

commit

A beautiful garden of our lives

Whenever I garden I find it difficult to tell the flowers from the weeds. Largely because it's a matter of personal preference. We decide what we want to cultivate and a weed is any plant growing where we don't want it. They're not inherently bad. They're not evil. They're not carnivorous triffids threatening to take over the world. They're just the wrong plant in the wrong place at the wrong time.

The problem with weeds is that they take up space where something else could grow. And therefore a beautiful garden doesn't often happen by chance. If we want things to flourish, we'll have to make room for them. We'll have to cut back the ivy and uproot the dandelions if more delicate flowers are going to see the light of day.

In the beatitudes that's what Jesus is doing. He's strolling through the garden of our lives like a master gardener telling us what to make room for. He sees the potential for beauty in the chaotic mess of our existence. He brings his face close to the fertile soil of our souls and spots good things we'd hardy noticed ourselves: a seed of openness, a shoot of mercy, a sapling of purity. No matter how insignificant or vulnerable they look, these are the attitudes to make room for.

When Jesus blesses the poor in spirit, the mourning, the meek and so on, he's not just saying go and do. He's not commanding us: "Go and be like this." He's watering the seeds of these beautiful attitudes. He's tending the potential for them curled up in us and making room for these fragrant attitudes to grow. He's not saying: these attitudes are missing and you need to get them. He's saying: these are the seedlings to cultivate if you wish to make a beautiful garden of your life. He's helping us separate the flowers from the weeds.

Heaven hovers

But it's difficult to view the eighth and final beatitude that way:

Blessed are those who are persecuted for the sake of righteousness,
    for theirs is the kingdom of heaven.

Jesus blesses the persecuted and it's hard to view the prospect of persecution as a rare flower waiting to bloom in us. On the whole persecution is something done to us, not something we do to ourselves. In fact, intentionally acting in ways that provoke persecution is hardly commendable. It would be more masochistic than moral, more self-harm than saintliness. If we're going to devise an experiment from this beatitude therefore we'll need to specify exactly what we're getting at.

Perhaps there's a clue in the fact that Jesus doesn't just bless the persecuted. The blessing doesn't rest on those who are attacked or ridiculed for anything whatsoever. But rather, the touch of recognition falls on those who are persecuted *for the sake of righteousness*. Heaven hovers over those who are willing to endure criticism, accusation, violence – persecution in whatever form it comes – for the sake of remaining true to what is good.

The temptation I suspect that comes to most of us when we encounter scorn or rejection is to respond in kind. We either harden ourselves in anger against our enemies or we adapt ourselves in some way. We change our minds. We redirect our intentions to ease the pressure. We make ourselves different to deflect the danger.

Either way we lose our grip on the kind of person we'd like to be. The future we were driving towards grows dim and fades. We allow our identity to be sculpted by people who oppose us. We allow who we are to be defined by those who don't like who we are.

This beatitude, therefore, is a gift from Jesus to people who refuse to betray themselves or fall in line with injustice at the first sign of trouble. He's extending a hand of affinity to those who stay true to the most loving and compassionate version of themselves no matter what is done to them or said about them. He's blessing us for not altering our peaceful intentions in the face of rejection or disappointment, for not changing direction with every gust of wind. His final beatitude is a comfort to those who remain committed to love even when exposed to hatred.

A bit of an anticlimax

I feel like I've gone on about this a lot, but let me say it again one last time: the people Jesus spoke to were generally on the defensive. They'd been forcibly commandeered into the Roman Empire and therefore felt that their identity as an ethnic group was under threat.

Blessing the persecuted was therefore a really unusual way for Jesus to finish the beatitudes. The eight of them possess a sort of rising dramatic tension. As Jesus blessed those who were pure and those who made peace, there's a good chance that his audience, carried by the swelling tide of energy, started to anticipate the great crescendo of blessing that would top the bill. I suspect they were hoping for something triumphant, something victorious, a rousing slogan for their future renaissance: blessed are the victorious for they will rule the world. But instead the persecuted get blessed.

It must have been a bit of an anticlimax. Jesus sits at the piano and plays the opening flourish impeccably, only to drop dead on the keys. It was a faux pas, a disappointing end to a promising strain of thought. It probably went down like a lead balloon. Many of the people he spoke to didn't want to be persecuted, they wanted to be in power. Just enough power not to be victimised ever again.

Jesus' talk of persecution could have been taken in different ways. They could have been words of comfort to people who'd been on the receiving end of imperial law enforcement. A healing balm for the true Jews who stood up for their ethnic identity in the face of a foreign occupying force.

But in all likelihood they had a much more subversive and controversial meaning. Jesus may not have been talking about persecution at the hands of their enemies, the Romans. That would come to his followers later. But to begin with persecution was likely to come to them from another source. People who adopted the way of Jesus and imitated his attitudes were more likely to be persecuted by their own people. He was therefore blessing those who would stand up for compassion among a people who, at that moment in history, were more concerned with conquest.

Fear prevents us loving

If you're anything like me, there are many good things in you that never get out. Many good intentions that never become actions. Many secret dreams of kindness that never see daylight. Who knows why we fail to act on our better natures. Perhaps we stifle them because we fear they won't be welcomed? We quash them out of fear of a hostile reception. There are times when our concern over what people might think prevents us from doing good. Could it be that fear prevents us loving?

It may seems strange to us that people who stand up for love, and compassion, and patience, and justice, and kindness, and understanding, and all manner of other good things, would be disliked. Surely these are the very things that gain universal applause and approval? It seems weird to think that being good could make us unpopular, especially if we've viewed being good as a way of being liked.

But living compassionately often presents us with a decision. Are we going to remain true to the compassionate calling of Jesus even if it means breaking ranks with people who expect us to be their allies and share their enemies? Are we going to back away from assassinating other people in conversation? Will we refuse to join in bullying the office geek? Are we prepared to live compassionately even if it makes us stand out? Which are we going to betray, the gang or our own commitment to love?

This is why righteousness can incur persecution. Goodness can become a flashpoint for hatred because it interferes with the way things usually work. And not just in personal relationships.

In organisations, ethical questions can get in the way of getting things done quickly. And in situations where time is money, goodness can be expensive. As a consequence, people concerned about the human cost of decisions often get accused of hindering progress or holding things up. They become the gadflies, the irritants, the obstructions in the way of progress, and therefore easily call down the impatience of any business or nation with a target to achieve. They become foreign bodies in the systems to which they belong and evoke an immune system response designed to remove anything that threatens the smooth running of the organisation.

This was the kind of persecution that frequently erupted around the band of disciples who first followed Jesus and it was only right of him to warn them of it. There are some places in the world today where following Jesus is still a dangerous occupation. Reading or writing a book like this one could get us arrested, imprisoned or tortured. To follow Jesus in a context like that is to know simultaneously that standing up for a different kind of world can call down the wrath of those who profit very nicely from the world as it is.

Jesus warned his disciples that they'd be in constant trouble if they followed him, but he also blessed them for it. He wasn't trying to induce their paranoia. He was just acknowledging that living a joy-filled, forward-moving, hope-inspired life has always attracted killjoys and defenders of the status quo – the petty tyrants and bureaucrats who'd rather see us silent than singing, and value compliance over compassion. Jesus was blessing those who were willing to endure dark times in their efforts to bring about a new day.

A circle in the air

But to this final beatitude, Jesus attaches a promise. He bequeaths something to us, like the final words in a last will and testament. We've heard it before and with it we come back to where we started, almost as if Jesus has drawn a circle in the air with his finger. Instead of giving us a check-list of blessings that roll past like the credits at the end of a movie, he's saying all eight beautiful attitudes hang together as a whole. He says of the persecuted, *theirs is the kingdom of heaven.*

We noted earlier that the beatitudes end as they began, with a promise of the kingdom of heaven. We also noted that this kingdom was the signature theme of Jesus' message to the world; that he spent most of his time in the public eye telling people that it had arrived and that they could be part of it.

But there was an apparent discrepancy in Jesus' touring first century Palestine with a message like that. He was saying that the kingdom of heaven was here, the God-stuff was on show, the seedlings of a new society were germinating. And yet, this wasn't entirely the case. The old ways continued. The Roman Empire continued intact. No new kingdom of any note had been birthed. If the kingdom of heaven was here, it was here in a sort of not-quite-completely-here kind of a way.

Jesus claimed to inaugurate the kingdom of heaven. He opened it to the general public. He cut the ribbon that let us into the theme park of God's dreams for the world. But even as we pass the gates we realise it's still being built. It's not complete. It's not done yet. We only have to take a quick glance at the world around us to know that a golden age has not dawned. If there is such an age to come, it hasn't come yet.

And yet here in the final beatitude we find Jesus placing the kingdom of heaven in the hands of people who are so committed to a better world that they're prepared to suffer for it. It's yours, he says.

Signs of a turning tide

This strikes me as a realistic proposition. A better world can only be brought about if people are willing to suffer for it. Especially when we look at the incredible problems that confront human life on the planet. They're a list of entrenched misery: the epidemic of HIV, poverty, drug addiction, human trafficking, child soldiers … the list could be extended indefinitely.

Not only are the problems monumental, but none of them are likely to change without someone somewhere enduring the pain of bringing the change about. In all the situations mentioned above, people are giving themselves painfully to the task of making some difference to the issues. I know some of them and I know what it's cost them. They've given their time, their lives, their money, their health, in the hope of making a difference. The world can only be changed if someone somewhere steps up to the plate and suffers to bring it about.

But is there not also something unrealistic in the idea that these deeply entrenched systemic evils can actually be eliminated? Believing that they can be almost amounts to believing the impossible. Because in the end, in spite of all our best intentions, nothing short of a miracle, perhaps a costly miracle, could heal the brokenness of the world as we know it.

I've steered away from talking about the miraculous aspects of what Jesus did: healing the sick, multiplying food, walking on water, stilling storms. I've not emphasised them because a lot of people find them hard to believe and because I don't want to look like a snake oil salesman telling you strange stories to entice you into agreeing with me. I wanted to avoid the idea that the miracles attributed to Jesus were somehow strategies to prove his divine credentials. They weren't. They weren't party tricks designed to say: see I told you I was God. Nor were they sideshows concocted to attract a crowd. They were a core part of his message that the kingdom of heaven was here.

The miraculous aspects of Jesus' life aren't incidental details to be brushed aside or ignored. They can't be explained away as tricks of the light or the imaginings of an overenthusiastic group of disciples. They're central to his message and without them it loses credibility. They're the symptoms of the kingdom of heaven being here. They tell us that the seemingly impossible feat of remaking the world has begun and that there are invisible resources available to those who work to see it happen. The miracles that spring up around Jesus and his followers, then and now, are the telltale signs of a turning tide. They give us hope for a new world in the making.

The ground breaking of a new world order

The great miracle in the biographies of Jesus is of course the resurrection – his return to life after three days in the ground. And this final grand miracle is anticipated in the eighth beatitude. Jesus lived this beatitude. He qualifies for his own blessing because he was persecuted and killed for the sake of righteousness. But this willingness to sacrifice himself became the foundation stone, the ground breaking of a new world order.

We could at this point get into an argument about whether the resurrection happened or not. It's tempting to list the pros and cons, to convince you on the basis of argument that it happened. And it wouldn't be wrong to try. Indeed, many people have written and debated this issue much more skilfully than me.

It wouldn't be inappropriate, but it wouldn't be true to the way I came to believe it myself. I came to believe in the resurrection of Jesus because of an experience of him in the present. The arguments, the thought and reasoning came later. What came first was an experience of God, a series of answered prayers and uncanny occurrences – a meeting of Jesus in the here and now.

This is the real world implication of the resurrection of Jesus: that he's no longer just a historical character, but can be met here and now. He's here. He's reading this with us. We can talk with him at any moment. We can be friends with God. That's what the resurrection means now.

And I guess the final beatitude challenges us to take our spiritual lives seriously. So seriously that we can live with looking stupid or deluded for the sake of knowing God. We'll never know how much we can change the world until we try. We'll never know how much God can help us until we ask for his help. Only those prepared to endure some degree of ridicule or rejection will fully understand what it's like to know God.

What wasn't quite so clear at the beginning, when we first started out in the God Lab, was that we were being gradually introduced to a God who had plans to make all things new. The beatitudes progressively induct us into a radical agenda for the overhaul of the way the world is. As we sit and make room for them, they change us and leak out of us, and change the people around us.

When we first start looking at them we don't realise that we're being groomed into a revolutionary. We're being radicalised. Not into explosive hatred and terror, but into unbreakable love and compassion. Sitting down with these eight words of Jesus makes us a little bit like him. They teach us to love against all the odds, as he did.

And so our final experiment is whether we can take seriously the news Jesus came to spread. If the kingdom of heaven, the God-stuff, the new society is waiting in the wings of this world, will we grab some of it? And what will happen when we do? That's the final and ultimate experiment in the God Lab. It's the graduating class. What happens when we give ourselves to God?

A good prayer

And so we reach the end.

It's difficult to know how to pitch this final experiment. Especially when it involves making some kind of commitment. It's difficult because I don't know what you're currently able to commit to. You may be ready to offer your life wholesale to the service of God, but equally you may not. I don't know what you believed when you started reading and I don't know whether you believe the same thing now that we're drawing things to a close. So how should we develop a final experiment around the notion of commitment?

There's a point in the biographies of Jesus where his disciples ask him how they should understand the parables he tells. Cutting a long story short, Jesus offers them a snappy phrase, a clue as to how we can make the most of any insights we receive from God. Talking about his own teaching he says, "According to the measure you use, it will be measured to you."

In other words, the amount of time, energy, attention and space we give to the words of Jesus will be more than repaid to us. Even a tiny glimpse of God, taken and mulled over, lived out and shared with other people, can become the keyhole through which we view the vast expanses of the things of God. All it requires from us is a degree of commitment to whatever God reveals to us.

It's up to you, therefore, to decide whether, through the experiments here, or by some other means, you've run into something of God: a moment of revelation, a conspicuous coincidence, a restored relationship, some prescient words, a supernatural occurrence, a dream or vision. Whatever it is, this experiment poses the question: is this something you would be prepared to stand by? Could you testify under oath to the light that has been given you, even if it's a fairly modest light? Can you make a commitment to the tiny seed of God planted in you? That's what our final experiment is about.

It goes like this:

Experiment 8:

Spot your commitment. I gave some examples above of possible experiences or revelations you may be able to point to and say, "It's a fact. That happened to me and I'm prepared to stand by it." It could be that what you can commit to is much vaguer than the examples I've given. Maybe you can commit to being more curious about God than you previously were, or to a rising hope that there may be a God. If so, feel free to commit to your curiosity or hope. If you don't feel you can currently commit to anything at all, feel free to sit this one out. We can meet up again at the end of the book. Otherwise, identify exactly what it is about God you can currently commit to.

State your commitment. If you are able to identify even a slight inkling of God that you can stand by or commit to, find some time alone to tell God what it is. A friend of mine who read this chapter said that the best prayer she could offer was: "I'm going to believe with everything I have that you're up there." She wasn't always sure, but that seemed like a good prayer to me. Try stating your commitment to God in a simple prayer. You may also wish to thank him for the light you've received and ask him to increase it. In a sense, you're blessing your insight, saying it's good, and thereby giving it some room to grow in your life.

Mark your commitment. In previous times, when people agreed to something, they often found some concrete way of marking it. They erected a standing stone to mark a boundary or put their family seal on a scroll. We still do something like this today when we exchange rings at a wedding ceremony. It's a material way of marking a particular commitment. You may want to think of a tangible way of marking your commitment to a glimpse of God. Some people would write a journal about it, others would do a piece of artwork or sculpture, or buy an ornament or jewellery to represent and celebrate their insight. Do something that will stand as a reminder to you of your experience of God.

Share your commitment. You may also wish to find someone to tell about your insight or newfound curiosity. To begin with, perhaps choose someone you think would be open and receptive to hearing about something like this. One of the first people I told about my early spiritual experiences was my religious studies teacher at school. I thought, of all the people in the world, he would know what I was going on about. (He didn't, but it was worth a shot). Tell someone you think would understand and then you may even want to tell someone you suspect may be more sceptical. Who you choose to let in on your commitment is up to you.

Watch your commitment. Having spotting it, stated it, marked it and shared it, the final step of the experiment is just to watch it. It can take time for our spiritual commitments to mature and flower in our lives. Sometimes it happens quickly, at others it takes months. Making a commitment is like planting a seed. It's then time to keep a look out for what God sends your way as a result of having taken a small but significant step in his direction.

Change of pace

A friend of mine decided to start following Jesus in his early twenties. I say he decided, but that wasn't the way he put it. He had no kind of religious background. His parents weren't believers, and his two brothers were sceptical. And yet there was something about Jesus that captivated him, that made a deep impression that wouldn't fade. He said he picked up the message of Jesus the same way he'd pick up a CD case in a music shop, just to take a look, and once he had it in his hand he suddenly realised he was holding the most important thing in the world.

One time Jesus told a story pretty similar to my friend's. Whenever he tried to explain what he meant by the kingdom of heaven, he often reached for imaginative ways of communicating it. Sometimes his biographers catch these moment of musing and record him saying to himself, "What is the kingdom of heaven like?" And then, as inspiration strikes him, snapping his fingers and saying, "Ah yes, it's like this …"

On this occasion, he compared the kingdom to a businessman or an antiques dealer scouring his local market stalls for a bargain. He finds, in the midst of all the bric-a-brac and ornaments, a pearl of priceless worth. So much so that he goes home and sells everything he has to buy it.

Jesus said that the kingdom of heaven is a bit like that. We can be oblivious to it and then one day accidentally run into it when we're not really looking. And when we do a double-take at what we've found we realise it's pure gold, the elixir of life, a pearl of great price. The meaning of life was lying around in front of our noses like a cheap toy. The stone on which we stubbed our toe was the foundation stone on which we could build a new life.

You probably noticed the change of pace in this final experiment. All the experiments needed some degree of commitment – just enough to believe that doing that or praying this was worth trying. But in the final exercise, commitment is the experiment. I guess, if my friend is right and the parable is true, then there comes a point in the things of God when searching ends and commitment begins.

The river can only carry us so far. We've negotiated the bends and the eddies. We've navigated the currents and the rocks. And now we hear the rumbling sound of the approaching falls. And we're left to decide whether we take the leap or not. Do we go where the river has carried us or do we paddle to the bank and save the plunge for another day?

When it comes to knowing God, we can only meander so far. We can only be carried some of the way before we're confronted with the need to commit. If we want to know him more, we may just have to start up a friendship.

exit

try

What exactly had I signed up to?

It's over two years now since I first put pen to paper to start writing the God Lab, and nearly ten years since I started gathering the ideas that led me to write it. It's been a long time in the making and things have changed a lot since the process began.

I started writing during one of the most disillusioned and confused periods of my life. A sort of early midlife crisis as I entered my thirties. The first few chapters no doubt bear the scars of that turbulence. It was a time of spiritual crisis that forced me to face some hard questions.

I was beginning to wonder what it really meant to be a follower of Jesus. What exactly had I signed up to all those years ago? And was it possible to put myself back again to the start? Could I stem the tide of growing cynicism and begin again as a disciple? Could I somehow rediscover the first love of Jesus I'd lost sight of?

I felt as if my spiritual life had entered a cul-de-sac. Having embraced a life of discipleship to Jesus enthusiastically as a teenager, I was starting to run out of steam. The passion that had gripped me in those early days was beginning to subside. A world that had previously seemed full and overflowing with hope and possibility started to look distinctly drab. I was world-weary. Too much water had passed under the bridge. Too many heroes had disappointed. Too many predictions of success had come to nothing. Too many selfish motives had been masked by spiritual language. My outlook was becoming jaded and cynical. Eyes that had sparkled with the light of enthusiastic fervour were growing dim.

Blessed are the dead ends

It was as if I found myself in a dark alley with my nose pressed up against the ugly brickwork of a dead-end. And for a time I despaired. I thought it was all over. I told close friends I was losing my faith. And then I told them I was just joking to make them feel better. I'd reached the end of the line.

And then something happened. Instead of collapsing into atheism as a default setting, something started to move. Something stirred in the depths of my being: a life that was greater than all my disappointments put together; an energy that could not be suppressed by my disillusionment; a light that the darkness could not extinguish. And before I knew it, it was erupting out if me: colour and energy and life and volume and inspiration and compassion and warmth and love and verve and possibility and ...

It was as if the dull grey bricks of my dead-end were suddenly spattered with vivacious colour. A bright mural of trees and birds and the glimmer of a distant sea appeared where there had previously only been grime-ridden cement. And more than that, as I watched the mural that burst out of me was alive. And there instead of a dead-end was a paradise to be explored. I stepped into the green foliage of the rainforest, to the call of birds and the distant lapping of waves. Barefoot through the grass and out onto the sand, I walked with gratitude, joy and wonder at every leaf and insect, and a boat rolling in the swell of the bay.

Somehow hope blossomed from my despair, and it's in this that I invite you to join me. This is the kingdom of heaven, a life that cannot be confined and will not be destroyed. This is what it means to know God. It almost persuades me to write a ninth beatitude of my own: blessed are the dead-ends, for they will become your delight.

Ready for some field trials

My writing was therefore really a prayer, a plea that somehow I'd find a way of carrying my devotion to God out of teenage fervour and into adult life. I started writing to change myself, or more accurately to be changed by meeting and contemplating Jesus again. And to a certain extent it worked. I end in a different place from where I began.

I crept into the God Lab cautiously, fearful that the caretaker would catch me and throw me out as a trespasser. But I'm leaving confidently with an appetite for adventure, wanting to test my newfound strength in the world beyond the laboratory, ready for some field trials. I've loved being in the God Lab, but it's not a place I can live. It's exhilarating to explore, but I'm not able to call it home.

I entered in the hope that I'd be changed. And I have. Maybe you have too.

Something to be tried

G. K. Chesterton once expressed a sentiment that comes pretty close to the pragmatic ethos of the God Lab. He said that Christianity hadn't been tried and found wanting, but rather found difficult and left untried. That about sums it up for me. If I had to choose a couple of words to express the experimental way of knowing God, I'd just say: *try it.*

Try spiritual openness and see if you meet God.

Try sharing your desires in prayer and see if you find comfort.

Try staying in the here and now and see if your grasp on life improves.

Try pushing for a sorted life and see if it satisfies.

Try giving up grudges and see if it frees you.

Try focusing your life and see if you become God-conscious.

Try working for peace and see if you find significance.

Try committing to what you know of God and see what happens.

These are the spiritual experiments you're invited to try at home. We've looked at them one by one and done our best to put them in a form that can be tried.

In bringing them to your attention I've sometimes felt like someone swimming in the sea, beckoning other people to come in too. I'm waving with a smile on my face, claiming that the water's lovely. And it is to me. But I know it may not feel that way when you first take the plunge.

Experimenting with God isn't always easy. It can be unfamiliar and uncomfortable and disconcerting. But I'm inviting you to try it anyway. And more than that, I'm trying to get across the idea that there is at least *something* to be tried.

A few experiments of your own

We also can't rule out the possibility that you found the experiments themselves unsatisfactory. Perhaps they didn't quite work the way you thought they would, or maybe they just didn't suit you. You didn't feel comfortable trying them out, or you wanted to do something different instead.

I share some dissatisfaction with the experiments. The beatitudes are full of richness and meaning, and it's laughable to think that any short list of bullet points could do justice to them. The words of Jesus are a hoard of spiritual insight and turning them into a to-do list runs the risk of selling them off cheap.

What I've called experiments here are really just things I've done with God over the last few years. I didn't call them experiments at the time. I didn't call them anything. I just found ways of praying and relating to God that allowed me to enjoy him. It was only as I started to write them down and give them to other people in workshops and training sessions that I started to think of them as spiritual exercises or experiments.

But, as I found, once you start experimenting like this you never quite know where you're going to end up. They often teach us far more than we expected. They don't just test the accuracy of each beatitude, they become vehicles for all kinds of insights into ourselves and our style of relating to God.

Perhaps you found this yourself? Through the experiments you learned a lot by accident, and not all about God. You discovered you didn't like to be alone, or always needed to be in control, or that you live for the approval of others, or whatever. And perhaps in the process, somewhere along the way, you also learned something about God? A mysterious sense of grace or acceptance fell on you. A prayer was answered. A relationship was healed. A dream guided you. Who knows what else.

There aren't any learning objectives in the God Lab. There's nothing you *should* have learned. And the only point I was keen to make was that it's possible to bring all our commitment, courage, curiosity and creativity to the task of knowing God. If we wish to.

There's a lot of freedom in the God Lab. There's freedom to improvise. So, if the experiments here haven't really done it for you, maybe it's time to design a few of your own.

We can still be friends

Ultimately, I hope you found this to be a kind book – not hectoring or aggressive, not arrogant or overweening, but a book you can play with – a book you can debate and disagree with. What you do with it is up to you. I leave that decision in your hands. You're free to shake your head and walk away, but I hope we can still be friends.

thanks

First off, I'd like to thank the four people who read through the entire manuscript and gave me detailed feedback. Some of my favourite bits of the God Lab were written in response to their comments and, thanks to them, some blunders were avoided. Thank you, Kate Southwell for allowing the book to disturb you and sending me your poignant reflections. Thanks also to Heather Tomlinson for casting your keen journalistic eye over the details – it all makes much more sense thanks to you. And thanks also to my father-in-law, David Dunlop, for being an enthusiastic and questioning reader, and for ensuring that I never fell too far into caricature. And thanks also to Gerald and Carol Dodd - proof readers extraordinaire. The good bits belong to you, the bad bits are all my fault.

I'd like to thank Stuart & Irene Bell, Senior Pastors of New Life Lincoln, for their unflagging support over the years. Thank you for giving me a chance and for making this project possible by directing me to Tim. Your generosity is wonderful and I'm not sure I always deserve it.

Thanks are due also to Tim Pettingale. It's fantastic to be blessed with a commissioning editor who really understands what I'm trying to do. You did. Thank you for championing the book at the point where I wasn't sure it was up to much.

I'm deeply grateful to Jim McNeish at House of Cantle for being such a good friend to me. You've been an incredible inspiration, a source of strength and wisdom. I'd like to think the gracious spirit of Cantle makes an appearance in some of these pages. The time when we write together draws closer ...

I also couldn't miss out the small army of friends who have surrounded us throughout the writing. My appreciation goes to John Manktelow, Colin Jordan, Phil and Emily Hearing, Dave and Jen Young, Cathie and Mick Paine, Jude and Simon

Wesley, Tom and Nic Law, Samantha Maw, Paul Quincey, Chris Shelbourne and anyone else I haven't mentioned who's shown an interest and offered some encouragement. Thanks too to Dale Newman and Adrian Toyne for praying throughout the latter stages of writing. Don't think I didn't know what you were up to. It was very much appreciated. And to Paul Timmins for being both organised and generous – a rare and helpful combination.

I'm also grateful to my trainers and colleagues in the UK Sensorimotor Psychotherapy DT group. You've accompanied me on this journey for the best part of three years, including the training weekend where I carried the manuscript round with me for five days like a protective parent. Thank you for all your warmth and loveliness. I'm sure you'll hear the echo of your voices in what's written here.

Several of my colleagues in the School of Psychology at the University of Lincoln have kept tabs on what I was up to and, while not always agreeing with what I was writing, have nevertheless kept up an interest. My thanks go to Professor Todd Hogue for being both encouraging and challenging in equal measure; to Drs Ava Horowitz and Rachel Bromnick for sharing a beautiful Seder with us; to Dr Paul Goddard for allowing me to blither on about this project for the last few years; and to Dr Kirsty Miller, my office mate, and one of the few people who knows why no one should ever swap chairs with me.

Paul, Joy and Finley Blundell have been an ever present source of support and laughter over the years. Thank you Joy for crying when you read it. Thank you Paul for putting up with yet another *nearly*. Thank you (or should I say *fanku*) Finley for teaching me the difference between a pair of socks and a couple of bats. I toast the mysterious One in whom our lives become inseparable.

Thanks are also due to my family: the Brethertons of Manchester, the Benvenistes of Wood Green, and the Dunlops of Ballymoney; Mum, Dad, Gill, Steve, Mati, Marco and Mary. Thank you for always being there, whatever the weather.

And finally, thanks to my delightful wife and boys: Marie-Claire, Leo and Tom. Life with you just gets better. Thank you for making the last few years the happiest. I love you.